The Corpse on
Clapham Common

Robert Christiansen Jr.
TRUE CRIME

The Corpse on Clapham Common

A Tale of Sixty Years Ago

ERIC LINKLATER

Macmillan

SBN boards: 333 00277 6

First published 1971 by
MACMILLAN LONDON LTD
London and Basingstoke
Associated companies in New York Toronto
Dublin Melbourne Johannesburg & Madras

Printed in Great Britain by
RICHARD CLAY (THE CHAUCER PRESS) LTD
Bungay, Suffolk

List of Illustrations

Preamble

IN January 1911, when I was not quite twelve years old, I was an avid, indiscriminate reader, and the daily newspaper gave me regular pleasure. In 1911 newspapers had more body, and were more richly flavoured, than the papers which cost a lot more today. Many events were more fully and frankly reported – especially events whose dramatic quality was made evident in a police court or the Old Bailey – and a paper's contents were not much diluted by gossip, its pages were almost unencumbered by advertisement. The great story of the Liberal Party's rise to power, and maintenance of power, in a battle for social revolution enlivened by Lloyd George's vituperation, made a deep impression on me, though as W. S. Gilbert so neatly predicted I had been born, and remained, 'a little Conservative'; and the coronation of King George V stirred loyalty in my scarcely adolescent breast. But what roused the liveliest excitement, and remained longest in memory, was the murder on Clapham Common of Leon Beron, which was discovered on New Year's Day; and from my warmly attentive reading of the trial that followed there emerged a stubborn conviction that justice had erred, and that Steinie Morrison, accused of the murder, was innocent of the charge brought against him.

I shall not pretend that indignation about a miscarriage of justice darkened my adolescence, nor that my memory kept alive the details of the trial for forty years. But when – in 1950, I think – I read Edgar Lustgarten's entertaining *reprise* of six famous and controversial trials for murder, memory came briskly to life again; for in that volume, called *Verdict in Dispute*, the second chapter retold, though briefly, the tale of Steinie Morrison.

The full, or judiciously edited account of his trial, by H. Fletcher Moulton in the series of Notable British Trials – published in 1922 – was out of print, and a long time elapsed before an Edinburgh bookseller was able to find a copy for me. But when at last I got it, and read it with some care, my schoolboy's suspicion of injustice was immediately revived. I was busy with other things, however – the world is too much with us, as even Wordsworth in the isolation of Grasmere discovered – and Steinie Morrison again receded into the little-regarded, or only darkly regarded, areas of my mind.

It was almost by chance, a few years ago, that I pulled Fletcher Moulton's narrative from a bookcase to read over my solitary breakfast: a working writer's day rarely corresponds with the nicely time-tabled habit of his house; and as my custom then was still to work late into the night, and get up late, I breakfasted alone and for half an hour or more read casually, for entertainment only, in the book I had happened to choose. But on that day the book held my attraction much longer than was usual. I went on reading it for most of the morning, and again and again I found my thoughts interjecting rank disbelief into what I read.

I happened to have on my shelves a few volumes of the *Annual Register*, and those recording the events of 1910 and 1911 sent me, within a day or two, to Edinburgh and the National Library of Scotland, where kindly people carried to my table ponderously bound collections of *The Times* and the *Illustrated London News*. I was struck – as who could fail to be? – by the curious contiguity, in time and space, of those other outrageous events that so closely neighboured the murder, on Clapham Common, of Leon Beron. In Houndsditch, a few weeks before, three policemen had been murdered by expert, ready gunmen of a sort wholly foreign to the English scene; and closely following the killing on the Common came that affair of extraordinary, sudden violence which was immediately christened the Siege of Sidney Street. When I read Fletcher Moulton for the third time I noticed a date, in the obscure history of Leon Beron, that had been curiously neglected, but which may be of some significance.

Until 1894 Beron had been living in France. In that year he, and other members of his family, fled from Paris to the refuge of

Whitechapel; and what, I asked, had happened in France, in 1894, to suggest, inspire or compel his flight?

I had some excuse for ignorance, because none of those engaged in the trial, on either side, had looked very far into the history of the mysterious Berons; and what I found – previously unnoticed though recorded in the *Annual Register* and *The Times* – finally persuaded me that it was worth my while, and possibly of advantage to truth, to retell Steinie's lamentable tale and set it in a context that would, to some extent, illustrate the temper and material environment of that age, and so, perhaps, prompt reassessment of his supposed guilt and of the dead man's contribution to it.

I believe Steinie to have been innocent of murder – of the brutal physical fact of murder – and though I cannot pretend that he was unaware of a plot prepared against Beron, or that he played no part in the prelude to it, it is possible, I think, to qualify his guilt by an assumption that he had not been told the dire purpose of the plot. If, moreover, Leon Beron was the victim, not of vulgar, homicidal robbery, but of old associates seeking reprisal for some unknown act of betrayal or dishonesty, then Beron himself was not quite guiltless of the deed.

And now, to conclude my preamble, I shall explain why I have chosen for the telling of the story – and its possible explication – a method that entails some repetition, and from a preliminary description of the murder on the Common harks back in time.

I looked for a background that would help to measure its impact on those who first read of it. I tried to make visible a minor period of history as it became evident to people who had to learn contemporary history from their reading of *The Times*, the *Daily Mail*, the *Illustrated London News* and other periodicals. To people of their sort – people, indeed, of all sorts – information has never come whole and entire. There is the first report of some startling or momentous event, and that may evoke memory of comparable or related events of which they have read in the past. Then will come more news, and first opinions may well be modified by it. News and knowledge come piecemeal – opinion is formed piecemeal – and I have tried to tell my story, not only as it appeared to its contemporaries, but in anticipation of an audience, not unlike intelligent newspaper-readers of sixty years ago, that will endure and enjoy a degree of repetition as the tale is again unfolded.

I have not tried to present a large, embracing picture of society in the now distant period of Queen Victoria's last years and the reign of Edward VII: that has been done more than once, most recently and most engagingly by Mr Priestley. But to illustrate the background of my story I have recovered a few samples of social gossip and commercial advertisement that may give the picture a chiaroscuro appropriate to the period.

The greater part, the bulk of the narrative, deals with the trial of Steinie Morrison. That was where my interest began, and the trial presents a drama of no less interest than the crime which occasioned it. It also reveals the extraordinary gulf that lay between the people with whom Steinie associated – the wretched population of Whitechapel, an alien society that lived in its own poverty and self-consciousness – and the solid bourgeoisie that provided jurymen to try him. In my account of the trial there is again much repetition. The progress of justice – if justice is to be achieved – is inseparable from the repetition of evidence, previously advanced, as it is examined by opposing counsel. I have, again deliberately, retained much of that sort of repetition because it is an essential part of the drama of the trial. But I have cut and confined it as far as I could without prejudicing the case for either side.

For my last chapter I have borrowed, from one of my betters, a story which – if it be found acceptable – will explain much that still seems darkly beyond explanation in the acts of violence which harassed the mind of England as 1910 turned into 1911. It is a story that was written, not after those events, but some years before them; and it may substantiate a belief, popular in 1911, that the Houndsditch murders, the murder on the Common and the siege of Sidney Street were in some way related. The author was a man of lonely genius, and when suddenly I remembered his story, and read it again, I thought: Here is a lucky find. Whether it can be taken more seriously I do not know.

ONE

The murdered man, Leon Beron

I

In the reluctant morning light of Sunday, 1 January 1911, Constable Joseph Mumford of the Metropolitan Police, on patrol on Clapham Common, discovered the body of a dead man among the furze bushes growing in a ragged clump on one side of the asphalt path which crossed the Common from the South Side to Battersea Rise and Lavender Gardens. The body was respectably dressed, horribly injured and apparently about fifty or sixty years old.

It lay on its back and its legs were crossed. It wore patent leather boots, a melton overcoat with an astrakhan collar, and tucked into the top of the coat was a black silk muffler, with red stripes, that covered the dead man's scalp. The night wind had been strong and squally, and dead leaves had gathered in so great a heap on one side of the man's neck that to Mumford it first seemed that the murderer must have made a cushion for his victim's comfort; but the brutality of the murder was not consonant with so fanciful a notion.

The head had apparently been battered with a heavy, jointed or jagged iron bar. There were multiple gross injuries on the right-hand side, the forehead was broken by five savage wounds, the left ear hung almost severed. Those were the wounds which caused death, and post-mortem examination subsequently showed that after death the body had again been assaulted: on both sides of the breast-bone the chest had been deeply stabbed, the wounds on the left-hand side penetrating the chest and abdominal walls, that on the right piercing the liver. The man's face was covered with blood, and closer scrutiny revealed that of seven superficial cuts two were symmetrical – there was one on either side – and looked like a pulled-out, elongated letter S. Those cuts had done nothing to hasten death, or make sure of it. They had been inflicted for another purpose. If the S-like incisions did indeed represent that letter, they might have been made either to identify the victim or leave upon him his murderer's signature; and if the resemblance to an S was fortuitous the savage scratching was surely proof of a hatred that even death could not expunge.

A bowler hat and a blood-stained pipe were found nearby. In a pocket were a rent-book and a letter addressed from a street off Commercial Road East. Though the circumstances of his death seemed to indicate revenge as a motive, the murdered man's other pockets suggested mere robbery: they were empty but for a halfpenny. It was ten minutes past eight when Mumford discovered the body, and the doctors' opinion was that death had occurred about six hours earlier.

On Monday, 2 January, *The Times* published, in two modest columns, the New Year Honours; and beside them, under a minor heading, news of murder on the Common. The police, it said, while still engaged on enquiry into the Houndsditch murders, had had their attention transferred from the East End to Clapham; and quickly a suspicion grew that there was some connexion between the killing of three policemen, a fortnight earlier, in a cul-de-sac behind Houndsditch, and the mysterious death of an unknown man, vaguely identified as a German or Russian Jew.

6

In mid-December the police had surprised a gang of foreign burglars – burglars who, perhaps, were anarchists under a criminous skin – and though, as housebreakers, the foreigners were far from skilful they were well armed and quick to shoot. The police, of course, had no weapons other than self-confidence and short wooden batons, which were no match for the burglars' automatic pistols. Cornered in the meagre lodging they had taken, the burglars broke out under a hail of shots, leaving behind, as well as three dead or dying policemen, one of their own gang who had been hit by an ill-directed bullet.

A reward of £500 was offered for information leading to arrest of the others, and three wanted persons were described. There was a woman, unnamed, aged twenty-six to thirty, in height 5 feet 4 inches, slim in build, with full breasts, blue eyes and brown hair; she wore a dark, three-quarter-length jacket and skirt, a white blouse, a large black hat trimmed with black silk, and light-coloured shoes. The two wanted men were Fritz Svaars and Peter the Painter, both of whom, according to the advertisement, were anarchists. Fritz Svaars was said to be twenty-four or twenty-five years old, in height 5 feet 8 inches or 5 feet 9 inches, a locksmith by trade, Russian by birth, who usually wore a dark melton overcoat with a velvet collar and an Irish tweed cap. Peter the Painter was older – twenty-eight or thirty – and perhaps a little taller. His complexion was sallow, his moustache black, his build medium, his manner reserved. Believed to be Russian, he wore a shabby black overcoat and a hard black hat which, presumably, was a bowler or *melon*. His real name may never have been discovered, or made known, but as 'Peter the Painter' he was elevated to one of the lower and murkier floors of our national mythology, and with the passage of time his fame grew until it acquired a fabulous political nimbus.

Between such sturdy desperadoes and the dead man on Clapham Common there was no obvious resemblance except their foreign origin and a common addiction to overcoats of melton cloth. But there was a good deal of xenophobia in England at that time, and distrust, dislike or fear of foreigners – when foreigners were less numerously domesticated in England than they are today – could do much to congregate them in an amorphous and anonymous horde whose shabby members were indistinguishable from one another. In the East End of London there were too many, and that nimiety was largely due to Gladstone's lofty mind and liberal policy. Gladstone, when Home Secretary, had made it known that any alien immigrant claiming to be a political refugee was to have the benefit of the doubt, and England became an asylum for both dissidents and undesirables.

For thirty years or more anarchists had attracted unfavourable attention, in part by the high-flying theories of Bakunin and Prince Kropotkin, but more urgently by the noise of their occasional bombs. In a leading article *The Times* had declared that 'the one subject which at the present moment interests the British public is that of the criminal or Anarchist alien'; in popular estimation the criminal and the anarchist were indeed indistinguishable, and theoreticians of the latter party did little to establish or clarify a difference. Anarchists, it was said, had found a comprehensive statement of their faith and purpose in three quotations: the first from La Fontaine, the second from Proudhon, the third from Diderot –

'Notre ennemi c'est notre maître.'
'La propriété c'est le vol.'
'La nature n'a fait ni serviteur ni maître. Je ne veux ni donner ni recevoir des lois.'

III

On Tuesday the third, with lavish generosity, *The Times* gave nearly five columns to an article on Tolstoy's last days and the contents of his will. He had died in November 1910 of an illness called 'nerve fever', which doctors treated in vain with wine, Vichy water and injections of camphor oil and strophanthin. For long a recluse at Yasnaya Polyana, he was in retreat from his vast estates, and on his way to Rostov-on-Don, when he fell mortally ill. The train stopped at Astapovo, and Tolstoy was given a room in the stationmaster's house. 'To escape, to escape!' he cried in his last delirium, and an editorial writer seized the opportunity to proclaim Britain's moral superiority to men of alien blood. 'The tragic story of Tolstoy's last days,' he wrote, 'awakens our deep sympathy, but Queen Victoria at 82, steadfastly pursuing her appointed task, presents a nobler ideal to normally constituted humanity than Tolstoy at 82, distractedly fleeing to a railway station under cover of night.'

That leader-writer was in luck, for the East End was already the scene of a new outrage which was bound to fortify distrust of foreigners and a complementary belief that England, by some miraculous dispensation, stood apart from, and above, the common run of humanity.

On 4 January, two days after announcing the Clapham murder, *The Times* published news, far more sensational, of a violent episode that must have done much to confirm suspicion that the typical foreigner was one who, in the doubtful privacy of a rented attic, habitually muttered, 'Je ne veux ni donner ni recevoir des lois.' In the discreet headlines of the age, no more than a column broad, *The Times* made known dramatic events:

FIGHT WITH ANARCHISTS

HOUNDSDITCH ASSASSINS

TRAPPED

TWO KILLED IN STEPNEY

SEVEN HOURS SIEGE BY SCOTS

GUARDS AND POLICE

A house in Stepney, to which the Houndsditch murderers had been traced, was surrounded yesterday by a large detachment of police and military. The criminals were fully armed and well supplied with ammunition. Shots were exchanged for nearly seven hours until the building caught fire and the men within either shot themselves or were burnt to death.

The rooms where the anarchists had found refuge were in an almost modern block of tenements – built in 1899 – in Sidney Street; and the siege of Sidney Street, as it was immediately entitled, acquired an added notoriety from the presence, in its latter stages, of the Home Secretary, Winston Churchill. To him both police and soldiers had cause for gratitude, for it was he who decided that the house and its occupants need not be taken by storm: the flames of its burning would do what was necessary, and no Guardsmen, no policemen, would be sacrificed.

When the fire was extinguished there was little left by which the stubborn, swift-shooting defenders of those blackened walls could be identified; but for reasons never made quite clear it was officially accepted, and allowed to be known, that neither of the charred and mutilated corpses found in the ruins was that of Peter the Painter, for whom the search continued.

IV

Five days later, on 9 January, newspaper-readers had their interest returned to Clapham Common. A man had been detained, on somewhat dubious grounds, and was held on the suspicion – not officially admitted – that he was responsible, wholly or in part, for the murder of the elderly Jew who had been beaten to death, stabbed after death, and marked upon the face with strange incisions.

The dead man had been identified, and found to be somewhat younger than he looked. His name was Leon Beron, and his age had been forty-eight. For three years he had lived in Jubilee Buildings, Jubilee Street, Stepney – a street which lay parallel with Sidney Street, quite close to it, and like Sidney Street ran from Mile End to Commercial Road East. With two brothers, a sister and their father he had come to London about sixteen years before. Since 1907 his father had lived in a home for the infirm, and both his brothers were poorly off. But Leon, though far from rich, had some property in Stepney and was generally well dressed. A widower 'of a reserved disposition', he was a man who made few friends. His brothers, Solomon and David, had been interrogated, and were absolved from suspicion. One or both had seen him, somewhere in Whitechapel or Stepney, in the late hours of Saturday night – only a few hours before he was killed, that is – but neither could offer any reason for his having gone to Clapham Common.

At the inquest on 6 January Solomon Beron, who was to attract more attention a couple of months later, was sworn in Hebrew fashion and gave evidence. He was, he said, a single man, of Russian birth; but his father – the old man now in a home for the infirm – had left Russia in 1864 and gone to Paris, where with a growing family he had lived for thirty years. He, Solomon, had no occupation, but lived in independence on his own means. He got some help, he admitted, from a sister who was still in Paris. In France, he said, his family had been well off.

His brother Leon, he declared, spoke no Russian and not much English, but knew French and Yiddish well. He was a sober man, and stingy. He collected his rents from nine houses in Russell Court in Stepney on Saturdays, receiving six or seven shillings from each. He had no bank account, but kept his money in his pockets. On a Saturday night, said Solomon, he might have as much as £12. (That was approximately a month's accumulated rents, but few of the witnesses summoned to the ensuing trial could be trusted to speak with accuracy about money.) Leon, moreover, wore a gold watch and chain, with a five-guinea piece attached to it for ornament: they, with whatever money he had, had been taken from his dead and mutilated body. There could have been no sexual motive for the murder: since Leon's wife died there had been no woman in his life. He, Solomon, had last seen his brother alive at 10.45 on Saturday night, when Leon, dangling his walking-stick, stood on the pavement in Fieldgate Street, as if waiting for someone. Fieldgate Street lay north of Commercial Road, roughly parallel with it, and ran eastwards from Whitechapel High Street.

Dr Joseph Needham, divisional surgeon of police for Balham, described the several wounds on the dead body. On the right-hand side of the skull a double blow had laid bare the bone, and left a loose tongue of skin between the lacerations. Great force had been used, and many blows struck. The chest and abdominal wounds had been made by knife or dagger after the body had fallen. Beron's cheeks had been covered with blood, and beneath the mask of blood were the S-like cuts which, said Dr Needham, could not have been accidental.

Dr Freyberger, who made the post-mortem examination, said the body was well nourished and muscular. He had taken photographs which showed the S-cuts on the face. They were two inches long, and only skin-deep. They were quite unconnected with the man's death.

21

It was again made clear that those mysterious incisions had only an approximate likeness to a printed S; more exactly, perhaps, they resembled the diacritical mark over the letter 'n' in such Spanish words as *cañon* or *mañana*. But they had not contributed to death, they had not been made accidentally, and in very many people – perhaps a majority of newspaper-readers – they woke a lively curiosity. Interest in them was not confined to England, and it was reported that an Austrian expert in criminal investigation had told the *Neues Wiener Tagblatt* that several cases of such disfigurement had been recorded by the Vienna police. To the criminal classes they were known as *slichener*, or traitor-signs; and the expert knew a woman who had been so marked.

In Graz, however, Professor Hans Gross, said to be an authority in criminal lore, offered a slightly different explanation. He told the *Neues Wiener Tagblatt* that a cut representing the letter S could just as well be the Latinised version of the Hebrew character *schihn*, the initial letter of *schlosser*, which, said the Professor, meant a police spy. A later suggestion, no more helpful, was that the letter so crudely inscribed stood for *spic*, the Russian word – or so it was alleged – for spy. No one, however, seems to have noticed that it could also have been the initial letter of the English word. But linguistic interpretation was of little importance in comparison with the doctors' evidence that the cuts were neither accidental nor contributory to death.

It was on 8 January, in Fieldgate Street where Solomon Beron had last seen his brother, dangling his walking-stick on the edge of the pavement, that the police arrested the man they suspected of murder, while refusing to admit their suspicions. He sat in a modest restaurant where he had had his breakfast – it was between nine and ten in the morning – and Mrs Cohen, wife of the proprietor, remembered him as a former customer whom they hadn't seen for some time.

She had a woman's reason to remember him, for he was tall and handsome, she said, dark and clean-shaven, with a good prominent nose; and he had conversational gifts above the average. He had been an actor and a singer, he told her, and had lately been living in Italy. He had finished his breakfast, and was leaning back at his ease, hands in pockets, when two police officers came in. The officer in charge was the well-known and redoubtable Detective Inspector Wensley, who, according to Mrs Cohen – but her memory does not always inspire confidence – seized his man round the neck, exclaiming, 'You are here!' To which the arrested man meekly replied, 'Yes, I'm here.' Three more detectives then entered the restaurant, and Wensley's captive was handcuffed. To the policemen surrounding him he said, again and again – if Mrs Cohen can be trusted – 'Don't put anything in my pockets!' When they took him out a large crowd had gathered, who followed the handcuffed man and his escort to the police station in Leman Street.

Two days later, on the tenth, he was charged, in the name of Steinie Morrison, at the South Western Police Court, with the murder of Leon Beron, the police offering only enough evidence to justify a remand.

V

At Morrison's trial, some two months later, there was police evidence that Leon Beron had had no connexion with the Houndsditch murderers; but that official statement did not convince all – and perhaps only a minority – of those who read it. The nearness in time of the outrage in Houndsditch, the Clapham murder and the fight in Sidney Street made many believe that some association may have existed between the scarred victim on the Common and the desperadoes who had killed the three policemen: they were, approximately, the same sort of people; they were refugees from Russia, Poland, Lithuania or some such tortured part of farther Europe. To a nearness in time, moreover, was added the nearness in space – the topographical proximity – of Sidney Street and the dismally narrow streets where Leon Beron had spent his days, and where – as later evidence made known – he had become acquainted, and perhaps even friendly, with Steinie Morrison.

From an obscure but criminal background Morrison was to emerge as a figure of uncommon character and great physical attraction. He was a handsome man with a powerful personality and a background darkly enigmatic, though some of its chapters were drably outlined by prison sentences. For a little while he attracted the same sort of interest as the more remote and mysterious Peter the Painter; and, as Peter the Painter's identity was never fully or satisfactorily established, so also did Morrison's guilt remain in doubt.

In the three events, associated by time and topography, there were three men whose antecedents were all unknown: Peter the Painter now seems hardly more substantial than a myth; Steinie Morrison was a burglar who had never shown a violent habit until he became, as was alleged, the murderer of Leon Beron; and who was Beron, the property-owner?

Russian or a Russian Pole by birth, his father had fled from Poland or Russia in 1864, and with his obscure family had lived darkly in Paris, attracting no recorded attention, until 1894. In Russian Poland, in 1864, there had been widespread unrest, the violence and persecution consequent on unrest; if Beron *père* had been politically active, he might well have had urgent reasons for removing himself and his children from the cruel probability of police interrogation.

Then, thirty years later, he had again taken to flight and left Paris in a hurry; or so it may be inferred. He brought his family to England, to London the universal roof against persecution, and for that exodus there must have been a reason.

What, in 1894, had happened in Paris that conceivably might have upset a long-established, and perhaps comfortably estab-lished, family of Russian refugees? Fear is the source of flight, and fear can infect all who belong to some racial or social minority when a member of it, by an act of outrageous criminality, has roused to equal violence the temper of the injured majority.

The President of France had been assassinated, and his murderer was a self-proclaimed anarchist. Others, known to be anarchists or to have associated with them, were immediately aware of danger, for anger like a flame ran through the streets of Paris and Lyon, and the virtuous mob went in search of victims. Only in flight was there much hope of safety, and those who could afford it fled.

Out of the wrath, confusion and muddled investigation that followed the President's death – the police seem to have been lax in enquiry – there emerged, in France, a belief that his murder had been planned in England where, it was known, some of the refugees whom Gladstone made welcome had shown less gratitude for hospitality than Gladstone expected. In London, too, in the early weeks of 1894, there had been a strange and shocking calamity that aroused a consternation which now seems almost as incomprehensible as the act of aborted violence that awoke it. The Metropolitan Police moved faster than their colleagues in France, and in what seems to have been a popular and well-attended anarchists' club in Whitechapel quickly found evidence that pointed to a projected attempt on the President's life. French suspicion may have been justified – perhaps London was indeed the temporary headquarters of international anarchism – and therefore it will be proper, as well as convenient, to begin, in London, a short account of the purposive but ineffectual acts of violence which, for about three decades, were directed against the established order of European society.

I do not propose to write a history of anarchism; but if the story I have to tell is to be given the emotional background it needs I must try to re-create or suggest the existence of a temper of anxiety which underlay the bluff confidence of England in the proudest years of its imperial power. For those who have forgotten – and those too young to have heard of them – I must bring to mind some illuminating or significant episodes that marred an era of great splendour, partial prosperity and relative peace.

But I shall be brief. I shall choose, from the annals of those years, only events which became known to people who dutifully read their newspapers and wondered with a growing concern if a pattern of assassination, and the unexpected explosion of home-made bombs, was likely to spread from European cities to their own overcrowded metropolis. I shall do no more than disinter, from forgotten files, a few instances of the anarchic violence that shocked a world which was too much inclined to congratulate itself on its good fortune.

TWO *The Autonomie Club in Windmill Street*

I

No crime had been committed. There had been criminal intention – that was obvious – but it had been defeated by mischance.

Mere intention, however, was enough to rouse an anonymous writer on the staff of the *Illustrated London News* to fury and indignation. 'An accidental death, hideous and horrible,' he wrote, 'but scarcely deplorable, as it deservedly ended the pernicious existence of one of those detestable criminals who plot the wholesale murder of the innocent, the destruction of private and public property. . . .'

The pace grows faster, his indignation cannot be restrained and his catalogue of turpitude becomes a little incoherent: 'and every other cruel mischief', he pants, 'that fiendish cunning devises for the vain purpose of terrifying society to overthrow all social and political institutions. . . .'

But there, as if breathless, he pauses and, remembering that his subject was 'accidental death', hurriedly concludes, 'took place on Thursday afternoon, Feb. 15, in Greenwich Park'.

Popular journalism in the 1890s was more emotional and full-throated than it is today, but even after allowance has been made for changing fashion the paragraph seems overcharged. From its involved and heavily loaded clauses the adjectives erupt as if they were the flying fragments of a moral indignation that fear had detonated; and if journalists anticipate or reflect the feelings of their readers news of the accident in Greenwich Park must have exploded like another bomb in the wintry air of February 1894.

The victim was Martial Bourdin, a French anarchist, and it was his own purpose that killed him. To us, who have lived for a long time under the distant menace of nuclear fission and fusion, the threat of an anarchist's home-made bomb may seem small indeed; but it was enough to horrify and frighten a world that profoundly respected the rule of law, and was enclosed in a prosperity that had no natural defences. It was a world that appeared to be self-confident, but its enormous riches were a burden and a responsibility as well as the source of much gratification, and latent enemies were near at hand in the poverty that surrounded it. It was a vulnerable world – its wealth was too widespread to be easily protected – and it showed itself aware of vulnerability in its nervous response to a guerrilla warfare waged by such desperate and simple creatures as Martial Bourdin. It seems unlikely, however, that he ever inspired fear in anyone until he killed himself.

French by nationality, an anarchist by conviction, Bourdin was a tailor by trade. Twenty-six years old, he had been born in Tours and lived for some years in America. He went to London about four months before his death to join his brother, who was also a tailor; and latterly had been unemployed. In some small way he must have attracted attention, for the police suspected him of concealing explosives; and in Greenwich Park he himself verified their suspicion. In the approaching dusk of a February afternoon he walked up the grassy hill towards the Royal Observatory which, built in 1675 'for the advancement of navigation and nautical astronomy', used to crown its summit. (Rebuilt in 1899, the Observatory was removed to Herstmonceux in 1948.) He was within sixty or seventy yards of the building when the bomb he was carrying exploded prematurely.

Perhaps he fell, perhaps the mechanism of his bomb was defective. The explosion, however, was loud enough to bring park-keepers in a hurry to the scene, where, under winter-stript trees, they found Bourdin, wounded deeply in many places, kneeling in a pool of blood. He was carried down to the Seamen's Hospital, and died there within the hour. He was a little man, hardly more than five feet in height, with blue eyes and fair, silky hair.

It was assumed that his intention had been to do such damage to the Observatory as a home-made bomb could inflict – 'to blow it up' was the popular phrase – and then escape to France; for he had, in gold and silver, about thirteen pounds in his pockets. As well as that considerable sum of money there were some recipes for explosive mixtures, and a ticket for a ball. He had no passport, for the liberal temper of Britain in the 1890s demanded no such document, but he carried his card of membership of the Autonomie Club in Windmill Street, off the Tottenham Court Road.

On the day after his death a trenchant leader in *The Times* declared that 'the moment when the professionals are apparently congregated in London, and are using this capital as the headquarters of international outrage' was not the moment for tenderness. About the presence in London of 'numerous active anarchists', there could be no doubt, said *The Times*; and on the following day, 17 February, another leading article commented with approval on a police raid at the Autonomie Club, where was discovered 'the headquarters of as pretty a collection of scoundrels as are to be found on the face of the earth'.

A narrow-fronted building, four storeys high with a dormer-windowed attic above, the Club was said to have been frequented by about a hundred foreign anarchists, of several different nationalities. Among the documents found by the police was a manifesto on red paper headed DEATH TO CARNOT. Marie François Sadi Carnot was the formally correct and dignified President of the French Republic. He still had four months to live.

What must be observed is that the England which permitted inordinate social difference, and stark poverty in the midst of ostentatious wealth, was equally tolerant of continental misfits and desperadoes. If it was blind to the indecent display of riches, it was deaf to the extremely anti-social opinions of some of the refugees to whom it gave sanctuary. In part, of course, its tolerance was due to the fact that the anarchists had previously exploded their bombs abroad. When one of them blew himself up in Greenwich it was necessary to exhibit disapproval; but though the Autonomie Club was raided, there was no attempt to expel from England all known or suspected anarchists. The complacency of an opulent world had been startled and stung, but composure quickly returned.

II

Thirteen years before Bourdin's death the Czar Alexander II had been murdered near the Winter Palace in St Petersburg, and in London a German anarchist called Johann Most published an article in which he defended the assassination. Lenient and liberal-minded though England was, that was going too far, and Most was sentenced to eighteen months hard labour. In France, within the next few years, such eminent leaders of anarchism as Prince Kropotkin and Louise Michel were imprisoned, and in the United States violent opinions were loudly uttered, and violent deeds were done. Several anarchist congresses were convened, and at Pittsburg in 1883 a programme for revolutionary freedom was based on the preliminary destruction, by all possible means, of what was called 'the existing class rule'. In Chicago there were some deadly encounters between working men and the police, and in 1886, at a meeting held to promote the idea of an eight-hour working day, several policemen were killed, and others wounded, by a bomb. For that outrage seven men were condemned to death, of whom two had their sentences commuted to imprisonment for life, and were later pardoned; one committed suicide; and four were hanged.

In the early 1890s there was a good deal of revolutionary propaganda in France and Spain, in which a man with the curiously sinister name of Ravachol was conspicuous. In Paris he protested noisily against the imprisonment of two anarchists, and threw bombs at the houses of the judge and prosecuting counsel responsible for their conviction. He in his turn was arrested, and presently the police discovered that he had lived a life of lurid violence. Born and brought up in desperate poverty, he had taken to a career of crime perhaps as a declaration of war against society, but perhaps, more simply, for sustenance and the support of his relations. He was a multiple murderer, confessing to five assassinations, and to more commonplace theft he had added graverobbing. He was sentenced to death, and under the guillotine died with a last cry of 'Vive l'anarchie!' Despite his proven and admitted criminality, Ravachol was immediately proclaimed a martyr by his fellow-anarchists.

At the beginning of December 1893, the anarchist Vaillant planned a very daring assault on France's elected government. From the upper gallery of the Chamber of Deputies he threw a bomb that struck a balustrade and burst, not on the floor of the Chamber as he had intended, but in the air. About eighty people were wounded, thirty of whom were Deputies, but none fatally. The President showed remarkable composure, and maintained order. All doors were closed, and the bomb-thrower was arrested. On 10 January, at the Seine Assize Court, he was found guilty of attempted murder and sentenced to death. When the judge reproached him for having tried to murder innocent men, he answered, 'There can be no innocent bourgeois.'

On the first day of 1894, under the sanction of a new law of public safety, the French police arrested in Paris, Rouen, Lyon and Le Havre rather more than 2000 men and women who were said to be 'prominent' anarchists. Prominence was not defined – no standard was erected against which their villainy could be measured – but on the following day at Saragossa the Spanish police took into custody a man called Franch, also described as 'prominent', and he was suspected of having planted or thrown a bomb in a theatre in Barcelona. With a true anarchist's distaste for confinement, and characteristic incompetence, Franch tried, but without success, to shoot himself; and then, in insufficient quantity, took poison.

In Barcelona a charge of dynamite had lately been exploded in the harbour, killing two and wounding several others; and, on the same day, the civil Governor was fired at and wounded by a workman who, on being arrested, proudly proclaimed himself an anarchist. Even in Zürich there was trouble; at the end of January a riotous mob attacked the Italian consulate, and after serious fighting was dispersed by the Swiss police.

In London on 3 February the Metropolitan police watched with some foreboding a large gathering of unemployed at Tower Hill. They formed up to march to Trafalgar Square, but were dispersed at Blackfriars. Or, more accurately, the majority were dispersed. A determined remnant reached Trafalgar Square, where wild speeches were made. Two days later the French anarchist Vaillant died under the guillotine in Paris. A week after that a bomb thrown into the café of the Terminus Hotel in the Rue St Lazare wounded a dozen people and demonstrated the resolute mood of the anarchist grenadier. He was a young man called Émile Henri, born in Barcelona of French parents. He was armed with a revolver, and in the gallery where he sat he held his immediate neighbours at bay, and wounded two or three of them, before lobbing his bomb on to the main floor.

Three days after the explosion in the Rue St Lazare, Martial Bourdin was killed by another in Greenwich Park; and observers of the European scene may well have thought they were witnessing a designed crescendo of violence. It is possible, then, to find an excuse for the excitement so noisily displayed by the anonymous journalist in the *Illustrated London News*, and to feel some sympathy with the leader-writer who believed that that was no time for tenderness.

III

The opinion of *The Times*, that the Autonomie Club in Windmill Street was 'the headquarters of as pretty a collection of scoundrels as are to be found on the face of the earth', was probably shared by most of its readers, and when the *Illustrated London News* declared the anarchists' purpose to be the creation of such terror as would 'overthrow all social and political institutions' there must have been many who contemplated the future with some foreboding. The *Illustrated London News*, then more than fifty years old, would not have had so long a life had it not reflected with fidelity a world acceptable to its readers in a society that, unlike its continental neighbours, did not oppose change with fury and indignation, but merely resisted it with a stubborn intention and deplored it when it became inevitable. In skilfully illustrated pages there survives the reflexion of an overfed and seemingly exuberant world – only occasionally disturbed, as if by indigestion, by a rising bubble of nervousness – that shivered to read of Martial Bourdin's death, shuddered to think of an explosion that might have shattered the Royal Observatory, and roundly condemned the little tailors who wanted to throw their ill-made bombs against its opulence.

On a page in the number published a few days after Bourdin's death there is a picture of the Observatory beyond a screen of winter-bare trees, with a cross to mark the spot where the dying tailor was found; there are others of the desolate little attic where he worked, of the close-set windows of the house in Fitzroy Street where he lived, and of the Autonomie Club with, for period value, a bowler-hatted, needy knifegrinder seated in his encumbered barrow in front of it.

In the same number a whole page is given to reproduction of a photograph of Miss Margot Tennant, newly betrothed to the Rt Hon. H. H. Asquith, Home Secretary; and on a preceding page it is fondly asserted that 'Society has not for a long time known such an agreeable flutter as that which has been excited' by the announcement of their engagement. Miss Tennant is described as a noted beauty who had shown an active interest in art and literature: 'She is believed to have been the original inspiration of the mysterious little coterie called "The Souls", in which Mr Balfour and other eminent personages have found affinity.' To Mr Asquith, the youngest member of the Cabinet, much praise is given, and popular interest in his second marriage is approved in the rather ambiguous assertion that 'The public cherishes a praiseworthy sentiment in these affairs, and seizes on any excuse for a romance'.

In contrast with Margot Tennant's portrait, so immediately recognisable, is the front cover which shows a Ministerial Dinner given by Mr Gladstone at 10 Downing Street. Mr Asquith is there, a thin, almost emaciated figure at one end of the table, and Gladstone, vaguely benevolent, may be identified by his central position; but except for them and one or two others the Cabinet Ministers are forgotten men.

Four or five neighbouring pages are filled with description and illustrations of the United Service Club, and a large engraving shows portraits of fifty of its senior members, of whom perhaps four remain in memory: Lord Roberts, Lord Wolseley, Sir Redvers Buller and the Duke of Cambridge. In a nearby article Andrew Lang declares that 'M. Gaston Paris is, perhaps, the most distinguished man of letters at this moment living'. He died in 1903; and today how many could account for his fame or defend his scholarship? How many have heard of him?

The world of seventy or eighty years ago was inhabited by people who served their day and generation, and with few exceptions left for their successors little evidence of their labours and no lasting memory of their voices and virtues, their public manners and private madnesses, their defeated aspirations. They were people who possessed curious furniture and elaborate ornaments, who bought almost as many bath-chairs as bicycles, and were constantly shopping for patent medicines and hair-restorers. The chattels and paraphernalia that filled their over-stuffed houses had – like our own – been designed for passing needs or fugitive fashion, and now seem almost as remote from our private plenishings as codpieces and Elizabethan ruffs. 'CIGARES DE JOY cure ASTHMA' states a small but confident advertisement, and comfortingly adds that they may safely be smoked by ladies and children.

On the same page there is a striking recommendation for a patent MASTICATOR (sixteen blades in one), to be used instead of a knife

for preparing chops, steaks, and all roast or boiled meats for mastication by mincing and pulping same on your warm plate, and so preserving all the nutriment. Those with Good Teeth should use the Masticator to save them; those with Defective Teeth should do so to assist Mastication, and those with Artificial Teeth should use it to prevent damage or breakage; in fact no dinner-table is complete without the Masticator.

On preceding pages it appears evident that Statham's Waterproofs were made to resist such torrential rain as recent years have rarely seen; and the Y and N Patent Diagonal Seam Corset was apparently constructed for the confinement of heroic figures of a sort that modern society neither nourishes nor would tolerate. There is, as yet, no advertisement for a motor-car, but the abundance of human power is clearly demonstrated by the variety and luxury of Leveson's Invalid Chairs and Carriages: Wicker Bath-chairs or Victoria Carriage, Bath-chairs with Hood and Window, fitted with small shafts for pony or donkey – they all require manpower, and a Carrying Chair doubles the requirement.

It should not be thought, however, that extravagance is encouraged. Messrs Ford & Company, at 41 Poultry, announce that Old Shirts may be Refronted at the cost of Three for Six Shillings (returned carriage paid); and Poudre d'Amour – equally suitable for the Nursery and After Shaving – costs only One Shilling in any of the shades Blanche, Naturelle or Rachel.

As well as the large engraving that portrays members of the United Service Club, there is a full-page picture entitled 'La Rose' by Arthur Burchett. 'La Rose' is a girl with wide and candid eyes, a warm but innocent mouth, and a nose which, boasting of good breeding, promises also impeccable morals. She is the sort of girl to read and appreciate the novels, published by Messrs Hurst & Blackett, that are advertised on page 246: *Hetty's Heritage* by Noel Dene; *Good Dame Fortune* by Maria A. Hoyer; *In an Alpine Valley* by G. Manville Fenn; and *Under the Red Robe*, the current serial by Stanley Weyman.

There is no need to suppose, nor reason for belief, that the literary works and painted pictures of our own time will live any longer, or enjoy a more lasting appreciation, than 'La Rose' and *Hetty's Heritage*. A few may endure, the vast majority will perish; but to acknowledge that – to admit that even contemporary fashions are ephemeral – does not diminish the sense of distance and total difference that seems to enclose, as if with their own atmosphere, so many things that were written and manufactured and offered for sale in the closing years of the nineteenth century. Twenty years after Miss Tennant announced her engagement to Mr Asquith the nineteenth century was separated from its wounded successor by a fracture in time almost as gross and decisive as one of those geological faults that in a distant past divided continents; and in some respects we are impassably remote from 1894.

In her *Autobiography* Margot Asquith quoted a letter from an anonymous 'well-wisher' in the East End of London. He reported that, at a meeting of the unemployed on Tower Hill immediately after the news of her approaching marriage, John E. Williams, the organiser appointed by the Social Democratic Federation, proposed that the unemployed should follow the example of people in the West End and send a congratulatory message to Mr Asquith. He moved:

> 'That this mass meeting of the unemployed held on Tower Hill, hearing that Mr Asquith is about to enter the holy bonds of matrimony, and knowing he has no sympathy for the unemployed, and that he has lately used his position in the House of Commons to insult the unemployed, trusts that his partner will be one of the worst tartars it is possible for a man to have, and that his family troubles will compel him to retire from political life, for which he was so unfit.' The reading of the resolution was followed by loud laughter and cheers. Mr Crouch (National Union of Boot and Shoe Operatives) seconded the motion, which was supported by a large number of other speakers and adopted.

In 1894 the unemployed received no compensatory pay for unemployment, and there was no such comfort for them as National Assistance. Poverty was real, and unrelieved except by the harsh shelter of the workhouse, the meagre sustenance of outdoor relief, the erratic help of charity and friendly societies managed by working people for their unfortunate neighbours: 'It's the poor that helps the poor.' In these circumstances the humour, and especially the good humour, of the unemployed on Tower Hill must rouse a wondering admiration; one cannot

readily believe that in a comparable situation today the unemployed would approve with laughter so genial a message to a
Home Secretary about to marry.

On Monday, 25 June 1894, *The Times* gave rather more than half
a column to description of a race, on the previous Saturday,
between the Prince of Wales's famous cutter *Britannia* and Mr
A. D. Clarke's *Satanita*, which the latter won by three minutes in
just over three hours, finishing in thick, dirty weather. On the
same day at Rugby – it was the school speech-day – the head-
master, Dr Percival, referred to his principal guest, Judge Thomas
Hughes, as 'Tom Brown'; and the Judge admitted 'exceeding
pride and pleasure' in his presence at the school which he had
first seen sixty years before.

On Saturday night, at White Lodge, Richmond Park, the
Duchess of York had been safely delivered of a son who was to
reign, very briefly, as Edward VIII; and at the Albion Colliery,
near Pontypridd in the Taff Valley, there had been a terrible
disaster in which 253 miners lost their lives. In the tremendous
explosion 120 horses or ponies were also killed.

At the Gaiety Theatre Sardou's *Madame Sans-Gêne* had opened
with Mme Réjane in the leading part: a review in *The Times*
filled most of a column. *A Gaiety Girl* could be seen at the Prince
of Wales Theatre, and at the Globe W. S. Penley was playing in
Charley's Aunt.

From France came the shocking news of President Carnot's
assassination. He was killed in Lyon while on his way from a public banquet to a gala performance at the theatre. His murderer's
name was variously given as Santo Caserio, Cesario Santo
and Hieronimo. Whatever baptism and his parents had done for
him, he was an avowed anarchist, twenty-two years old, born in
the province of Milan but lately living in Sète, on the coast of Bas
Languedoc, where he had worked in a baker's shop. He had
quarrelled with his master, and before leaving Sète he bought, from
a gunsmith, a dagger that cost him five francs.

Accounts of the assassination vary. One witness declared that
Santo, carrying a large bouquet, ran after the President's open

carriage, jumped up and, pulling a dagger from the bunch of flowers, stabbed the President through the ribs. Another said the carriage had stopped, and among the crowd pressing forward to shake hands was Santo, who took Carnot's right in his left, and held it while he stabbed him. Santo narrowly escaped being lynched, and his clothes were torn to pieces by his infuriated neighbours. He was a poorer man than Bourdin, for the police found only sixty centimes in his pockets.

The dying President was carried to the Préfecture, and the windows of an overheated room were thrown open. Immediately the room was filled with the dazzle and glare and detonations of a grand display of fireworks, and Carnot died amid the monstrous gaiety of the Catherine Wheels, Roman Candles and Bengal Lights that had been bought to do him honour and whose display no one had remembered to cancel.

Carnot was a good man, apparently of simple character and domestic tastes, of unquestioned integrity, and in a country tormented by ephemeral policies and short-lived ministries he had been regarded as the only stable element in France's government. But the anarchists hated him because he had refused to exercise his prerogative of mercy to save the lives of Ravachol, Vaillant and Henri – men who were generally regarded as criminals, but whom the anarchists esteemed as heroes and martyrs.

Two of the many anarchists-in-exile in London were reported by Le Matin to have spoken in defence of the murder. Alexandre Cohen, a Belgian expelled from France, said, 'It is not an assassination, it is an execution. Ravachol, Vaillant and Émile Henri are avenged.' And in 'her London retreat' Louise Michel declared, 'This execution is more than a simple act of justice. In Carnot a whole class, the whole bourgeois world has been struck at. . . . Anarchy will once more have deserved well of mankind, for love of mankind is the sole object of anarchy. Individual revolt is the prelude of the grand plebeian revolution whence social harmony will emerge.'

Louise Michel was for some part of her life known splendidly as the Red Virgin of Montmartre. Born at the château of Vroncourt, daughter of a housemaid and a son of the house, she lived with ardour and recurrent heroism. A fiery patriot during the siege of Paris, she later joined the National Guard, offered to shoot Thiers and magnificently suggested that Paris should be destroyed in expiation of its surrender. She was with the Communards in their last stand in the cemetery of Montmartre, and after several periods of imprisonment – at one time she was sent as a convict to New Caledonia – she found refuge in London. She lived until 1905, and at the age of seventy-five was still preaching anarchism and revolution when she died in Marseilles.

She was a heroic woman whose energy and retention of a persistent faith are much to be envied, as private possessions, though their public expression helped no one. It is matter for bewilderment, however, that a woman whose intelligence, in some ways, was abundantly evident should live so long and still believe that social harmony could be the product of a 'grand plebeian revolution'; or, indeed, of any revolution. To her, Carnot's assassination was an attack on 'the whole bourgeois world'; a blow struck at those who, as Vaillant had declared, were never innocent. But the writer of a leader in *The Times* saw the murder as 'evidence of that modern revolutionary theory which aims at the destruction of that which is common and fundamental to all systems of government ever known among men'.

In France and Italy popular opinion agreed with *The Times*, and in defence of traditional systems of government – of that authority which is the core of government – there was rioting in many cities. Angry demonstrations against those known or thought to be anarchists showed clearly that the great majority of people detested violence – especially philosophic violence – in spite of Louise Michel's assurance that it was an act of love. The riots provoked a new exodus from the Continent, and yet more anarchists fled to London.

In France it was widely believed that Carnot's death had been plotted in England; and that there were grounds for suspicion cannot be denied when one remembers the raid on the Autonomie Club, and the discovery there of the manifesto on red paper that, as early as January, had threatened death to the President. His assassin, Santo Caserio, maintained throughout his trial, and after it, that he had left the baker's shop in Sète, and gone to Lyon, with the deliberate intention of killing Carnot in revenge for the execution of Émile Henri and other anarchists. On 3 August, the second day of his trial, he was found guilty 'without extenuating circumstances', and sentenced to death.

A few days later thirty French anarchists, of whom two at least would now be described as intellectuals, were indicted in Paris for criminal conspiracy to destroy social institutions by acts of violence, but twenty-two were acquitted, and only three, who were burglars as well as anarchists, were sentenced to long terms of imprisonment. From Milan it was reported that Santo's mother had become insane, and his brother, who kept a wineshop, had committed suicide. In the early morning of 16 August Santo was beheaded by the guillotine, and a correspondent of the *Illustrated London News* blamed the French *Police politique* for gross ineptitude. According to him they knew of Santo's presence in Sète, where he had made no secret of his intentions; but they did nothing at all to safeguard the President or hinder his assassin.

V

Unimpaired, as it seemed, by bomb or dagger, the bourgeois world and its institutions resumed what still appeared to be a normal way of life and their appropriate functions. At the Palace of Versailles M. Casimir-Périer was elected President of France, and at Windsor the Russian Czarevitch and the Archduke Franz Ferdinand of Austria were guests of Queen Victoria. The Prince of Wales opened the new Tower Bridge, and a great procession of boats filled the river to celebrate the occasion. Henley Regatta began in fine weather, and splendid illuminations prolonged festivity into the warm darkness of a summer night.

In the *Pall Mall* magazine Meredith's novel, *Lord Ormond and His Aminta*, reached an end, agreeable to its readers, when Lady Ormond eloped with the schoolmaster; and George Bernard Shaw wrote philosophically in the *New Review* about his play *Arms and the Man*, which no one understood except himself and the dramatic critic Mr Walkley. Another distinguished critic, Clement Scott, observed that Sarah Bernhardt, as Marguerite in *La Dame aux Camélias*, played with so tremendous an effect that her audience was utterly exhausted: 'When that magnificent death-scene was over, those who had witnessed it could scarcely speak to one another. They felt as limp as rags.' At the Lyceum, where Henry Irving and Ellen Terry were playing in Tennyson's *Becket*, the same critic thought they had never been seen 'to better advantage'.

There was cholera in St Petersburg, and in the United States Eugène Debs was arrested when the policy he had sponsored in the American Railway Union had such disastrous consequences that it seemed to presage a general insurrection of working men in Illinois, Montana, Idaho, Wyoming and other western states. Troops fired on the rioters, and some were killed. Enormous damage was done before order was restored and the threat of chaos averted. Even angrier than Debs and his railwaymen were the great eastern empires of China and Japan, and war between them was imminent in that long and almost unknown appendage of farthest Asia, the peninsula of Korea.

Readers of the *Illustrated London News*, however, were encouraged to contemplate scenes typical of the English way of life, which must have gone far towards persuading them that England was almost immune from foreign catastrophe because England – if one's views of it were carefully chosen – was different from the rest of the world. It was richer, and happier, and morally better. In the issue of 14 July, for example, there was a double-page picture of the Ladies' Meeting of the Toxophilite Society in Regent's Park; and no other country, one feels, could have matched or even challenged such an army of tall, slim, taut and lovely, trimly dressed maidens and young matrons as blossomed from the London turf.

A week later the Queen was at Aldershot, where the Duke of Connaught was leading a march-past of nobly attired, plumed and bemedalled soldiers, and high-stepping horses. In that issue, moreover, there was a full-page photograph, taken at Montagu House in Whitehall, of the Dowager Duchess of Abercorn, on her eighty-second birthday, at the centre of her living descendants, who numbered 101. Her eldest daughter, the Dowager Countess of Lichfield, was there with thirteen children and thirteen grandchildren; the late Countess of Durham was survived by thirteen children and fifteen grandchildren; the Duchess of Buccleugh had contributed a modest seven. In those days not only the poor were fertile; a vigorous and almost untaxed aristocracy could also afford fecundity.

Yet doubt remains about the state of Britain, and the health of even its more prosperous classes seems not to have been good. Everywhere patent medicines were advertised, and countless thousands must have lived in daily reliance on Carter's Little Liver Pills. Popular, too, were Cockle's Antibilious Pills, for which a testimonial had been written by Captain Fred Burnaby of the Blues, famous for his ride to Khiva: an elegant giant of a man, Burnaby suffered from constipation, and on his travels had met a desert sheikh, similarly afflicted, whom Cockle's Pills had miraculously cured. As irresistible in Arabia as in the Home Counties appears to be the underlying theme of the advertisement, and that is the explicit commendation, to far-travelling Englishmen and their wives, of Aspinall's NEIGELINE for the skin: 'Equally beneficial in its effects in the cold of Russia and Canada and in the extreme heat of India and Africa.'

Perhaps as remarkable, and even more useful, was COCA-TONIC-CHAMPAGNE. That was a combination, by the actual champagne-growers, of their *Grand Vin Brut* with pure coca-leaf extract, and the tonic thus obtained was said to have been universally prescribed 'to sufferers from Influenza, Insomnia, Nervous Breakdown, Neuralgia, and all forms of Neurasthenia' at the very reasonable price of eighty-four shillings for a dozen quart bottles.

One had supposed that nervous breakdown was a malady characteristic of our own distracted society, and little known in earlier times. But in the last decade of the nineteenth century military officers had problems that may have caused much anxiety, and perhaps Coca-tonic-champagne was prescribed for them. In August the German Kaiser reviewed our troops at Aldershot, and it was generally agreed that there had never been a handsomer parade on Laffan's Plain. Drill was flawless, dressing impeccable, uniforms were brilliant. But out of a division numbering more than 19,000 men only some 12,000 were available to go on parade, and the low field-state of the cavalry was due to the unfortunate fact that 13,000 troopers had only 6000 horses. Many a conscientious colonel must have suffered from insomnia, and taken what he could to cure it.

31

In the journals and periodicals of the age, the great world is proudly chronicled and splendidly illustrated. The ills and ailments of a larger and more general world are indicated, often with point and vigour, in the advertisement pages which generously offer remedies for them. Directly or indirectly the wealth and power and physical frailties of Britain are made obvious in a hundred ways. News, in any detail, of the working classes, the poor and the dispossessed, is more difficult to find, and the many refugees from the harsher disciplines of Germany and France and Italy are invisible in the warrens of Whitechapel. The enormous and seemingly unaided destitution of the 1890s must have had mitigations of some sort, and it may be that a majority of refugees lived their full term of years; but most of them lived out of sight except for an occasional brief appearance in some obscure police court.

Note has been taken of the exodus of frightened people from France after the assassination of President Carnot; and of those who came to London all but a very few must remain anonymous. But in 1911, nearly seventeen years after their flight, two members of that curious family called Beron emerged from obscurity and, for a little while, were familiar figures wherever newspapers circulated. One of them, who may have been mentally deranged, excited contemptuous laughter; the other acquired notoriety after he had been battered to death by cruel and seemingly revengeful hands on Clapham Common.

Leon Beron may have been murdered for the money in his pockets and the gold watch he wore; that was the view agreeable to official eyes. But so simple an explanation was not generally welcomed, and the deliberate, post-mortem, double scarring of his cheeks cannot be ignored because the writing was not easy to read.

At the trial of Steinie Morrison no one drew attention to the fact that the Berons had fled from Paris in the year when panic followed the President's death. No one suggested that old Beron and his sons may have been among those whom a sense of guilt, or an inquisitive policeman, sent hurrying to the nearest railway station. It was a curious omission, for if counsel for the defence had let fall, with apparent innocence, a conjecture that the Berons had been politically active in France, the theory of murder-for-revenge would have gained new plausibility. And the conjecture was not improbable.

Perhaps Leon Beron and his murderer were both related, by sympathy and association, to some of those violent men whose intemperate actions so luridly disrupted the world's complacency. The dead man on Clapham Common may have been a victim of international anarchism, his murderer an agent.

THREE   *The Siege of Sidney Street – The burning house*

I

FROM the distance in time of 1970, the years 1910 and 1911 look remarkably like the year 1894; and one can say with some confidence that their resemblance to 1894 is closer than any likeness to the present day.

It must not be assumed, however, that the last decade of the old century, and the first of the new, were uneventful; and the frivolities that decorate some preceding pages need graver addition even for a passing reflection of the age. In his fourth administration Gladstone failed to achieve a settlement in Ireland, and at the age of eighty-four finally retired. Income-tax rose to eightpence in the pound, and a coalition government of Conservatives and Liberal Unionists brought in such progressive measures as a Factory and Workshops Act to enhance safety and sanitation in England's dark Satanic mills; a Conciliation Act to permit the amicable settlement of industrial disputes; and a

Workmen's Compensation Act. But its liberal programme was interrupted by the outbreak of war in South Africa, and that lamentable conflict exposed some grievous deficiencies in the training and physique of British soldiers, and in the professional ability of their generals.

Fiscal policy was threatened with rupture when for the prevailing system of free trade Chamberlain proposed the substitution of 'fair trade'; and in 1902 and 1905 foreign policy took on a new and tangled look as treaties of alliance were made with Japan for a safeguard against the apparent menace of Russia. For a little while, indeed, war with Russia seemed not improbable; a Russian fleet, on its way from the Baltic to defeat in the straits of Korea, lost its bearings and binoculars in the North Sea and opened fire on a flotilla of English trawlers. That was in 1905, and in the same year the Kaiser Wilhelm II made a flamboyant intervention in Moroccan affairs, and his open challenge to the Royal Navy – he had declared that Germany's future lay upon the sea – was perhaps made more significant by his claim to have established a Divine Alliance for the better pursuit of policy.

In 1906 a great Liberal revival provoked a long and famous controversy, and brought about social and political changes which, at the time, seemed almost revolutionary. Though it would be an exaggeration to suggest that Britain was shaken by the birth-pangs of the Welfare State, it is not inaccurate to say that much of Britain was deeply shocked by the behaviour of those fiery young radicals, Lloyd George and Winston Churchill, whose assault on the old and still respected body of *laissez-faire* had all the appearance of a political rape.

The general election of that year gave the Liberals a majority of 84 over all other parties and, in alliance with Labour and the Irish Nationalists, a working majority of 356. Two years later Lloyd George succeeded Asquith at the Exchequer, and his first budget provoked fierce dissension between Lords and Commons. Death duties became oppressive, alcoholic liquors were more heavily taxed and the unearned increment of landed property was made subject to very painful dues. The new Chancellor spoke contemptuously of the House of Lords – 'They toil not neither do they spin' – and privilege turned pale and dukes empurpled in

35

their wrath. Political power passed to unaccustomed hands, and the old structure of society was slowly being undermined. Income-tax rose again, to one and eightpence in the pound; but the visible shape of society – its manners and habit of life – remained unchanged, or revealed such changes as only those within it could easily detect.

The old Queen had died in January 1901, and Edward VII, who had been sixty when he succeeded, died in May 1910. But his funeral had shown that Britain was still an empire whose power none could deny, though before long it was to be hotly disputed. The late King had loved life with uninhibited warmth, and doted on pageantry; his people, in exuberant reciprocity, had loved him, and in his lifetime no pageant had exceeded in magnificence his splendid funeral. The principal mourner was the heir to the empire he had bequeathed: King George V, a sailor by training, by nature dedicated to duty and by accident of royal birth Defender of the Protestant Faith and Emperor of India, whose remote and disparate faiths he equally protected. Following him, behind the royal and imperial coffin, came the Emperor of Germany, the Kings of Greece, Spain, Portugal, Denmark, Norway, Belgium and Bulgaria; the Archduke Franz Ferdinand of Austria, the Prince Consort of Holland, a flock of lesser royalties and that ebullient Quixote of American politics, lately President of the United States, the scholarly rough-rider, Theodore Roosevelt.

Nor did the empire diminish under George V. Rather was its importance emphasised by the extraordinary collapse of other monarchies during his reign. In his biography of the King, Sir Harold Nicolson reminds us that 'he succeeded his father on May 6, 1910, and reigned for almost twenty-six years. During that quarter of a century the world witnessed the disappearance of five Emperors, eight Kings, and eighteen minor dynasties. The British monarchy emerged from the convulsion more firmly established than it had been before.'

The year of the new King's accession still wore a late-Victorian complexion, though different impulses dictated much of its business. Winston Churchill established labour exchanges to reduce the recurrent misery, for casual labourers, of being temporarily out of work; and, having promised and devised a scheme of insurance against unemployment, he saw it become law in 1911 as the National Insurance Act. A couple of years earlier Churchill the modernist – a champion of social reform – had been closely and unpleasantly involved in conflict with those rival champions, Mrs Pankhurst and her daughters. By then the adult male population of Britain, with few exceptions, enjoyed the parliamentary franchise; but no woman was allowed to vote. To remedy this injurious disability Mrs Pankhurst had founded the Women's Social and Political Union in 1903. It soon became militant, and in 1908, when Winston Churchill sought re-election in North-West Manchester, the Suffragettes harried him in an offensive characterised by much violence and appalling noise. One evening in the Free Trade Hall, 'Miss Christabel Pankhurst, tragical and dishevelled' – they are Churchill's own words – 'was finally ejected after having thrown the meeting into pandemonium'.

That was the start of a guerrilla campaign, outrageous in many ways, offensive to at least half the country, often ingenious but in lamentably poor taste, which lasted half a dozen years until the outbreak of war in 1914. Then Mrs Pankhurst emerged as an ardent patriot, and transformed her fighting party into an organisation for national service. Though more boisterous than their Victorian mothers, the Suffragettes were 'new women' in only a restricted sense, and most of them, when not in prison or chained to the railings of some pavement in Westminster, preserved behind superficial infraction of customary behaviour a stable Victorian respectability.

In 1910 the battle for Liberalism was renewed in heat and fought with bitterness. There were two general elections, in January and again at the end of the year, and in January the Liberals lost 104 seats to the Conservatives, but with Irish and Labour support Asquith retained a working majority of 124. That result, with which Asquith himself appeared to be content, was accepted as a popular expression of approval for Lloyd George's Budget and the new taxes to be levied on death, potable spirits and landed estates; and the Budget, previously rejected, was passed by the House of Lords at the end of April. But the Government intended also to limit the power of the House of Lords by means of the Parliament Bill, which was designed to secure to the

37

House of Commons unrestricted authority in the matter of finance, and a predominant authority in all legislation. To the Conservative or Unionist Opposition it seemed that Asquith's reduced majority did not warrant his taking measures that might alter the balance of the constitution – the King had promised that he would, if necessary, create new peers in numbers sufficient to force acceptance of the Parliament Bill by the Upper House – and it soon became evident that Asquith would again have to canvass the electorate and seek its will.

Parliament was dissolved on 28 November, and presently the country resounded to the clamour of new speeches and old arguments, the consequence of which was the return of Asquith and a government pledged to enactment of the Parliament Bill with a majority that scarcely altered his previous margin of power. And before the last and farthest results were known there was news of an outrage so shocking, and of a sort hardly known to Britain, that most of the country lost interest in politics and gave all its attention to the horrifying tidings of a multiple murder in the dark East End of London.

The story of the Houndsditch crime, told briefly in Chapter One, must now be related a little more fully and with, perhaps, an appreciation of its impact sensitised by reminiscence of the politics and social scenery which were its background. I make no pretence to have drawn a full or fair picture of late Victorian and Edwardian England; but I have, I think, recreated a view – or some part of a view – that must have been familiar to an average newspaper-reader of the time, and it is that reader, in his horror and indignation, of whom we should think when we hear again the staccato pistol-shots that shocked the darkness of Houndsditch and England's complacency.

II

The first report, in *The Times* on 17 December, was short and vague. Several policemen were said to have been watching a house at Exchange Buildings in a cul-de-sac behind Houndsditch, in the expectation of making an arrest. The house was immediately behind a jeweller's shop, belonging to a Mr Harris; and the suspects were two men and a woman, of foreign appearance, who had been in residence for some little time without becoming friendly with their neighbours, though they had attracted attention by the noise, of banging and hammering, that they made.

The Times drew a pretty distinction between Houndsditch and its immediate neighbourhood. A staff-writer explained:

> Houndsditch, which runs from North to South between Bishopsgate and Aldgate, forms, with its continuation, the Minories, the dividing line between the City of London and the district lying to the East which is commonly called White-chapel, and is the great receiving ground of the poorest class of aliens from Eastern Europe. Houndsditch itself is highly respectable; it is mainly a street of shops, including some very large ones.

But the narrowness of the boundary between respectability and wild rascality was about to be revealed to the doomed policemen who were watching the house in Exchange Buildings and listening, perhaps with some foreboding, to the noises echoing behind its walls. According to one account, they were suddenly surprised by two men who rushed out, pistol in hand and shooting wildly; and an alternative version said police had entered the house and encountered their armed assassins on the stairs. The foreigners escaped, and one of the five policemen, all reported wounded, died soon after admission to hospital.

That story was quickly amplified and amended. The house, which consisted of a single room on each of three storeys, had been taken by a foreign woman at the beginning of December, and despite their reticence the new tenants had advertised their presence by sounds which could only have one meaning. They were trying to break through into the shop of Mr Harris the jeweller, and if they had attacked in the right direction they would probably have succeeded in burglary as well as in escape. But the first hole they opened was in the wrong wall, and their neighbours, who had been in no hurry to bring in the police, at last reported noises which by then, one supposes, had become a nuisance.

On the night of Friday, 16 December, Sergeant Bentley and Constable Martin, of the City of London police, stood in Houndsditch at the door of the jeweller's shop. The sergeant had heard for himself the noise of attempted intrusion, at the back of the shop, and having sent another constable to telephone to Harris, and tell him to bring his keys, he and Martin walked round to Exchange Buildings where other police officers waited. There was some discussion about which door to approach, and when Bentley knocked at Number 11 there was a brief delay before the door was opened, for a few doubtful inches, to show a man who seemed to understand very little of what was said to him.

He was told to go and find someone who spoke English, and went upstairs. Bentley followed, and in the darkness at the back of the ground-floor room another door, that led into a yard, was thrown violently open. From there, and from the stairs, came sudden revolver-fire. Sergeant Bentley was mortally wounded, and Constable Martin, retreating from the street-door, either tripped and fell or prudently threw himself to the ground. The gunmen, still shooting, ran out, and before disappearing killed or wounded the four unarmed officers who waited in the cul-de-sac. Sergeant Tucker, after twenty-five years' service, was shot twice and died in hospital where Bentley died later. Constable Choate was killed in a maniacal fury, for his body and legs showed no fewer than eight bullet-wounds; and Sergeant Bryant and Constable Woodhams were also wounded. Only Constable Martin escaped unhurt.

It remains uncertain how many foreign miscreants there were in the house at Exchange Buildings, but by the following day their desperate little company was reduced by one, despite the somewhat perfunctory services of a Dr Scanlon. He, an assistant to Dr Bernstein in the Commercial Road, Whitechapel, was called on at half-past three on Saturday morning by two young women who told him there was a man at 59 Grove Street who was 'very bad' – meaning seriously ill or gravely injured. Dr Scanlon went with them, but on the way to Grove Street one of the women ran off and was not seen again. The other took Scanlon to number 59, where a light shone from an upper room; but the street-door was locked, the lower windows shuttered. They knocked, and no one came. Then, after long delay, the door was opened by someone unseen, and the doctor – apparently unperturbed by the lack of welcome – struck a match to light a dark passage and a narrow stair.

In a room on the first floor a badly wounded man, fully dressed, lay on a bed. He had been shot, he explained, by a friend with a revolver: shot in the back, but only by mistake. Scanlon examined him and found, under the front wall of his chest, a bullet which had entered from behind. The name of the wounded man was Gardstein. He refused to let himself be taken to hospital, and the woman who had called on Scanlon returned with him to Commercial Road where, for her patient's comfort, she was given a narcotic.

Gardstein died that day, and in the room were found a loaded Männlicher automatic pistol, with two loaded magazines nearby; more ammunition elsewhere; burglar's tools, dynamite and blowlamps; and some pamphlets which the police described as 'Nihilistic literature'. In another room, in a house in Gold Street, Stepney, where Gardstein had lodged, more papers and weapons were found, and the police were satisfied that he and his associates were members of an anarchist group which had planned to live by burglary.

The whole country was deeply and truly shocked by the gross brutality of the outrage – the dead body of Constable Choate, with eight bullet-wounds in it, was evidence of his murderers' savage temper – and much was made of the disparity between policemen armed only with short wooden truncheons, and foreign anarchists who carried automatic pistols.

To most people living in the congenial innocence of Britain such weapons were quite unknown, and the mere thought of automatic fire created horror and apprehension. It was, indeed, both right and proper to condemn, with all possible severity, the murderous shooting of policemen whose ultimate weapons – even less lethal than a wooden truncheon – were only the tolerant acceptance, by the general populace, of its need of uniformed guardians; and the policemen's own liberal recognition of the constitutional and Christian fact that criminals, in Britain, had the right to be apprehended without bloodshed. But it would be wrong to suppose that assault on the police, and public shooting, were quite unknown in England.

Much can be discovered in the byways and obscure places of history that contradicts a prevailing temper and, as it were, the official character of the long age that lasted from the heyday of Victorian power to the golden summer of 1914; and one of the oddities of behaviour that, from time to time, rudely perforated, but failed to dislodge, the smooth integument of contemporary life had occurred – as *The Times* recalled – 'at Tottenham less than two years ago'.

Justifiably perturbed by the Houndsditch shootings, an editorial writer, commenting with some irascibility on the alien criminals who found London so convenient a harbour, remembered the insanely bloody day when two of England's unwanted guests had 'planned to commit a robbery in the open street at half-past nine in the morning, and in the course of what followed shot dead a constable and a boy, severely wounded three other constables, and some fourteen bystanders. They just pulled out revolvers and ran down the street firing at all and sundry.' Though Tottenham could not protect itself against the eruption of such violence, its inhabitants were in no doubt that the gunmen were of alien origin; and *The Times* cannot be accused of unjustified complacency when it asserted that 'the British criminal never does a thing like that'.

It might well have gone farther and commented, with comparable satisfaction, on the story of an anarchist meeting that one of its reporters brought from somewhere near Brick Lane in Whitechapel. At that meeting a Spaniard walked on to the platform, revolver in hand. The chairman explained that their guest, a comrade from Barcelona, could not speak English, but would demonstrate the best way of using a revolver. The Spaniard then fired over the heads of his audience, at a target at the other end of the hall, 'and gave a really pretty exhibition of shooting'. His demonstration was followed by a dance – and even the most unbiased commentator could have said that British political meetings were never like that.

Britain was still an island, and happily conscious of its insularity. There were signs, indeed, that its historical isolation might become less relevant when some new forms of locomotion had been developed, but few people realised the significance of Mr Sopwith's achievement, news of which on 19 December got small attention in comparison with the sensational tidings from Houndsditch. Sopwith had flown the Channel from Eastchurch to Beaumont in Belgium, a distance of 170 miles. It was less than two years since J. T. C. Moore-Brabazon had become the first British citizen to fly an aeroplane in Britain, and already there were about fifty certificated pilots in the country. But probably more pride was roused, more interest excited, by the *Mauretania*'s maiden voyage to New York, a swift passage of less than five days, through very rough seas, to a rapturous welcome.

Britain was a maritime nation, still guarded by its surrounding tides; and in the third week of December 1910 it was insistently reminded of the fact by a great gale blowing from the south-west. There were cries for help from wrecked or labouring ships, and lifeboats were putting to sea to rescue sailors in distress. There were floods from Severn to Thames. The island had its share of rough weather, but its fortunate people could usually point to a foreign origin for any exceptional display of rough behaviour.

Within a very short time they were again to be shocked and alarmed by the violence of continental criminals, and one of the men wanted for the murders in Houndsditch was about to acquire a sinister but shadowy fame that would keep his name alive, in popular memory, for many years. The two named and described by the police were Fritz Svaars and 'Peter the Painter'; and a notion was propagated, or grew by consent, that Peter the Painter was especially dangerous. In the subsequent trial of Steinie Morrison, Steinie's counsel called him 'the arch-fiend of them all'; but offered no reason for that monstrous elevation. By the police of Marseilles Scotland Yard was told that Peter the Painter had lived there from May 1908 till December 1909, and had been, by turns, a medical student and a house-painter. Born in Pskov in June 1883, he had arrived in Marseilles from Oran, in company with known Russian terrorists, and had once been arrested in a police raid. The French police sent a photograph of him, and the information that by them he was known as Piatkov Peter. When he left Marseilles, at the end of 1909, he had gone to Evian-les-Bains. In that dossier there seems nothing to persuade even a somewhat emotional barrister that Piatkov Peter was the arch-fiend of anarchism, but that was the reputation which – perhaps gratuitously – he acquired.

The police, gravely angered by the murder of their comrades, made urgent and vigorous search for Peter and his fellow-criminals. With a thoroughness of which Conan Doyle would have approved – and which makes them obvious contemporaries of Sherlock Holmes – detectives disguised themselves as shoe-blacks, Jewish pedlars and street-hawkers to comb the East End; but made no perceptible progress until shortly before the New Year came in. Then they received information that Fritz Svaars, a man named Josef and perhaps one or two others were at 100 Sidney Street, off the Mile End Road. Number 100 was one of a block of eight three-storeyed houses that stood, somewhat isolated, on a forty-foot road opposite a row of mean, two-storeyed houses behind which were Messrs Mann & Crossman's Brewery and the London Hospital.

Before the attack began a preliminary sortie was made to rescue the innocent occupants of the house. In the early darkness of 3 January a few carefully chosen constables, trained to arms, took post at 4 a.m., while Inspector Collinson and two sergeants, Hallam and Leeson, made a cautious entrance and brought out several people who lived on the ground floor and the top floor. On the first floor the door into the front room was locked; it was known, or strongly suspected, that the newly arrived lodgers lay there, and the question naturally arises: why did the police not force their way in?

The answer is that in Houndsditch these men, or others of their sort, had been surprised in the darkness of early morning, and under cover of darkness had shot their way out and escaped. It had been decided that in Sidney Street no action should be taken until daylight could aid the attack. It is not known if the gunmen were wakened by the police, but they made no attempt to interrupt the evacuation.

On the ground floor lived a man called Fleischmann, described as a costume-maker, with his wife and four children; and on the top floor were another married couple and several children. Fleischmann also rented the middle floor, and eighteen months before had let its front room to Betsy Gershon, a tall, dark woman who wore glasses and was said to be well educated: she spoke Yiddish, Russian and a little English. Her husband, formerly a wig-maker, was somewhere in Russia, where he worked as a silver-plater; but not, apparently, with much success, for Mrs Gershon said that she sent him money.

She in her turn had sub-let her room to the two strangers – the impression grows that everywhere in the East End there were casual lodgers, gipsies of the slums – and perhaps she had been compelled to do so. One of the men she knew as Josef, the other not at all. She said they had insisted on staying, and had frightened her. On the night before the siege they had made her take off her skirt and shoes, to prevent her running away, and in dangerous proximity to them she had slept in the room behind theirs, which Fleischmann used as a stockroom.

The first shots were fired as day broke, or soon after. They came from the windows of the first-floor front, and Sergeant Leeson, shot in the chest, cried out, 'I'm done, Jack!' Sergeant Hallam was luckier, and escaped with a bullet-hole in the rim of his bowler hat. A doctor arrived, only half-dressed, and the anarchists began to fire at anyone they saw. More police arrived, to the number of three or four hundred, but their purpose was not assault. They had been summoned to protect the local inhabitants and control the mob of excited spectators who already were beginning to assemble.

What ensued was a fantastic, a luridly improbable episode in the long history of London, but the scale of it should not be exaggerated. It was at half-past nine that military aid was called for, and three-quarters of an hour later a small detachment of the Scots Guards arrived. They found it impossible, or impractical, to force an entry into the back parts of number 100, which were protected by 'courtyard walls and other obstructions', and a few marksmen took post with armed policemen in front rooms of the small houses opposite. Others remained at either end of the block.

It was when Winston Churchill, the Home Secretary, arrived before noon to assume personal control of the proceedings that the story acquired some fictitious decoration. Throughout his life Sir Winston rarely failed to add lustre to the actions that he shared or initiated, and as a lamp to envious moths that lustre attracted the jealousy and ill-will of all who disliked him. He was accused, on this occasion, of transforming a criminal incident into a noisy drama by ordering to the scene Guardsmen in excessive numbers, and the pomp of the Royal Horse Artillery. But the facts were otherwise.

The Scots Guardsmen, who had been called out before Mr Churchill's arrival, numbered only twenty – a junior officer, two N.C.O.s and seventeen Guardsmen – and the Horse Artillery's small thirteen-pounders, though seeming incongruous in a London street, could very conveniently have breached the walls of a house which, fiercely defended by strongly armed and desperate men, might have had to be taken by assault, with inevitable and perhaps heavy loss of life for the soldiers and policemen involved.

Of the very large number of police assembled, every constable was needed. The siege attracted huge crowds of onlookers, who for their own safety had to be controlled. Most of the firing came from the opposite and opposing windows – criss-crossing the narrow no-man's-land of that sombre street – but the anarchists had an apparently inexhaustible supply of ammunition, and bullets struck brick walls in a flurry of red dust or, deflected, went singing over dark pavements. Recklessly the noisy spectators pressed in towards the centre of the stage, tried perilously to find window-seats with an unimpeded view – the fugitives from troubled parts of Europe were, perhaps, masochistically attracted by the staccato impact of automatic fire, the warbling whine of a ricochet – and conspicuous among them were very many girls and women, who showed no sign of fear. Because the swarming sightseers, on either side, were polyglot and largely alien, the police, in the early hours of the day, were doubtful of their temper. Would they show sympathy with the besieged gunmen? Would their sympathy become active, and hostile to men in uniform?

The possibility had to be admitted, but in the event was loudly disproved. The polyglot crowd allied itself – noisily and beyond dispute – with the police. The aliens of the East End appeared to reject all loyalties to their tormented homelands, and become Londoners in sentiment.

46

At about half past twelve smoke was seen to be coming from the back parts of the besieged house. How the fire started is not known, but it was thought that a gas-pipe had been cut by a bullet. It was a quarter past one when fire engines arrived, and those on the outskirts of the crowd applauded the helmeted men who came at a gallop to subdue the flames; and then, with amazement, watched their inactivity before the blazing growth of the fire.

The battle continued and policemen in disguise moved through the jostling throng, while others kept watch in the yard of the nearby brewery and on the roof of the Rising Sun, a public house at the corner of Sidney Street and Commercial Road. But the Fire Brigade still waited for orders. The Home Secretary had been quick to perceive means of saving life – the lives of London policemen and Scots Guardsmen – by letting fire maintain the offensive against their enemies. Neither they nor the brass-helmeted men from the galloping engines went into action until it became evident that the flames which consumed the house had also dealt with the anarchists who had so stoutly held it.

When the house was burning hard, it was said that two shots were heard from within, and it was supposed – or the guess was hazarded – that one of the gunmen had shot his companion, then himself. The firemen aimed their hoses at the blaze, and with the assault of water came the gunners and drivers of the Royal Horse Artillery from their barracks in St John's Wood: trotting fast through the streets, they had covered the distance in forty minutes. There was nothing now for them to do. Within its walls the house was falling down.

The casualties of an action fiercely fought on the one side, prudently controlled from the other, were two policemen and four Scots Guardsmen with bullet wounds; four bystanders wounded; and six firemen injured, one very seriously. Within the blackened ruin of the house were found two charred and dis-membered corpses, a dozen Mauser and Browning pistols and several sewing-machines that had fallen from the upper storeys through burnt and disintegrated floors.

Both the bodies had been decapitated, and what remained of one – according to *The Times* – was a charred mass; of the other, the arms below the elbows and the legs below the knees had disappeared. A coroner, Mr Wynne Baxter, was more gruesomely picturesque. 'All that has been found of one', he said, 'is contained in a handkerchief.' Nothing remained by which the bodies could be identified.

The murderers of the policemen killed in or near the respectability of Houndsditch were never brought to trial; and there was no proof that they had died in Sidney Street. Three men and a woman, arrested for murder, were indeed charged at the Central Criminal Court in May, but no evidence was found to convict them. Dubof, Peters and Rosen were the names by which the men were charged, and all were acquitted. The woman, called Nina Vassilieva, was found guilty of being accessory after the fact, and sentenced to two years' imprisonment.

The accused, Steinie Morrison

FOUR

THE Houndsditch murderers may have escaped punishment, or
they may have died in the battle of Sidney Street. They certainly
evaded trial and judicial execution, and the blackened fragments
of humanity that remained in a burnt-out house could not be
identified. On two counts the police, and justice itself, had been
frustrated, and at the trial of Steinie Morrison there was, perhaps,
an unavowed determination that the mystery of Leon Beron's
death should not remain unsolved, nor his murder go unpunished.
The law required a victim, and to some it may still seem that
Morrison had been cast in the leading role in a drama of revenge.

On 9 January – the day after he had breakfasted in a Jewish
restaurant in Fieldgate Street, and submitted to handcuffs and
Inspector Wensley – he was formally charged with murder before
Mr John de Grey at Leman Street Police Court, and though these
initial proceedings need not be described in detail – most of what

49

was said in the Police Court was repeated at the Old Bailey – they offered a prelude to the major drama which predicted its manner and mood in noise and confusion.

The dead man's brother Solomon complained that he had been pauperised by litigation with a firm of solicitors – an irrelevant complaint that he did not try to substantiate. He hotly denied that his brother, 'a retired gentleman' and a widower, had ever been an anarchist; but threw some doubt on a subsequent rumour that Leon had been cheated of a fortune of £26,000 by his statement that the murdered man had previously worked, in Paris, as a locksmith. He had no knowledge, said Solomon, of Fritz Svaars or Peter the Painter, and with startling reliance on the credulity of the court declared that he and his brother, whom he saw every day, had never discussed the murder of the three policemen.

When Edward Abinger, who had been briefed for the defence, suggested that both Leon and Solomon had been in contact with the police, when they were investigating the Houndsditch crime, Solomon's denial was again vigorous; and brazenly he attempted to incriminate Steinie Morrison.

'My brother', he said, 'told me that Steinie Morrison invited him to Sidney Street.' And pointing his finger at the prisoner exclaimed, 'I am sure of it! That is the murderer of my brother.'

The magistrate, de Grey, told him, 'You must not say that.' And Solomon replied, 'I say it! Since my brother has been missing in the restaurant, he' – Morrison, that is – 'has been missing too.'

Then the prosecution suffered an embarrassing reverse. A witness called Eva Flitterman, a girl dim-witted perhaps, but apparently honest, swore that on 1 January she had seen the prisoner wearing on his watch-chain a five-guinea gold piece. That had been the conspicuous ornament on Leon Beron's watch-chain, and if Eva Flitterman had told the truth, or even persisted in her story, it would have been difficult for anyone to pretend belief in Morrison's innocence. But Eva had made a mistake, and admitted it. Her father, on his watch-chain, wore a gold coin which she had believed to be a five-guinea piece, and the pendant on Steinie's waistcoat had, she thought, resembled it. But her mother had since told her that what her father wore was a two-guinea piece; and from Eva's bewildered mind the fancied resemblance promptly disappeared. There was, in fact, a pendant on Steinie's chain, but it was only a Kruger half-sovereign.

A second witness also recanted. He, a boy called Rosen, had said, on oath, that he had seen the prisoner on the streets at half-past one on New Year's morning; and on some previous occasion had seen him carrying a revolver. On further reflexion, however, he admitted a mistake about the time at which he thought he had encountered Morrison; and prudently remembered that he had never seen him with a pistol. He said also that Solomon Beron had threatened him with grievous harm if he retracted his evidence.

Neither witness was called at the trial, and the circumstances in which they were induced to testify may possibly be explained by an assumption that some unknown policeman had yielded to an excess of zeal.

II

The trial opened in the Central Criminal Court, the Old Bailey, on 6 March, before Mr Justice Darling. Mr R. D. Muir led counsel for the Crown, Mr Edward Abinger was the prisoner's leading counsel.

Muir and Abinger were not only opposed in purpose, but contrasted in temper: the former a man of stern and forthright habit, logical, relentless and stubborn in attack; the latter more easily excited, emotionally involved in the defence of his client and apt to yield under the long strain of the trial to nervous irritation and occasional impertinence to his lordship.

Mr Justice Darling was famous for his wit, the elegance of his manner, his literary ability, his tendency to levity. He had often taken obvious delight in the opportunities to prick pomposity that heavy-handed legal argument recurrently offered him. He cannot have found any pleasure in presiding over a trial for murder set against the squalid poverty of Whitechapel, but he was remarkably patient, scrupulously fair and only once yielded to the temptation – and then quite properly – of rebuke by epigram.

A jury was sworn, and Morrison, formally charged with the murder of Leon Beron, was asked, 'Are you guilty or not guilty?' To which he replied, 'My lord, if I was standing before the Almighty I could give but one answer. I am not guilty.'

Opening the case for the Crown Muir described with clarity the discovery of a dead man on Clapham Common, the nature of the lethal wounds – inflicted, he said, by a crowbar or jemmy – and of those dealt after death. The body had been robbed, and in due course was identified. Beron, living in a very poor way, had for several years spent most of his time in a restaurant kept by a man called Snelwar. But Snelwar used to give Beron gold in exchange for silver coins: the rents, presumably, that he collected from his nine tenants in Stepney. According to Snelwar the dead man was commonly in possession of £20 or £30 in gold, which he kept in a wash-leather bag pinned to an inner pocket of his waistcoat. His waistcoat was further decorated by a gold watch and chain, to which was attached a £5 gold piece.

As the case proceeded there was much talk about money, and it is not unfair to say that most of the witnesses took a romantic rather than a realistic view of it. Money was something infinitely to be desired, rather than something of which they had much practical experience. They wanted to know about it, and seem to know about it; but, when they spoke of it, it became apparent that they saw it floating beautifully in the air, rather than lying solidly on the counter of a bank, or comfortably in their pockets. But Muir accepted, without any show of doubt, Snelwar's evidence of the dead man's portable wealth; and it may have been true that the habitués of the restaurant had regarded Leon Beron as a walking treasury.

In money and valuables, said Muir, he had on his person about £50 or £70, and the evidence would show that some pretext had been used to persuade him to go to Clapham Common – a district with which he had no known connexion – in order to be robbed and murdered. He made it clear that in his opinion robbery was the only motive, and all the redundant wounds were inflicted because the murderer, having robbed his victim, dared not take the smallest risk of leaving him alive. He made no reference to those wounds which did not contribute to death, nor tried to fill in an obvious gap in his argument. If the murderer's motive had been simple robbery, and if in fact Morrison was the murderer, why had he gone to the trouble of escorting Beron all the way to Clapham Common, thereby giving several cabmen the chance to identify him on that improbable journey? There were squalid lanes and dark corners within easy reach of Snelwar's restaurant where a man could as secretly and more expeditiously have been beaten to death. To some nearby destination, through some black alley, Beron could plausibly have been lured; but what lure was it that took him, at two o'clock in the morning, for a walk across the Common if, between him and Morrison, there was no junction of interest other than £30 and a gold watch?

Beron, said Muir, was a regular customer at Snelwar's restaurant, and for a fortnight or so before his death Morrison had frequently been seen there with him, apparently on such friendly terms that he had been allowed to hold and examine Beron's gold watch. On 31 December they both spent the greater part of the day in the restaurant – it was called the Warsaw – and in the evening Morrison gave to a waiter a parcel to keep for him. Snelwar's little daughter asked what it was, and Morrison replied, 'A flute.' But the waiter– or so Muir and the waiter averred– knew that to be false, because the parcel felt and weighed more like a bar of iron. Before midnight Morrison reclaimed his parcel, and he and Beron left the restaurant together.

At several places in the East End, said Muir, they were both recognised by people acquainted with them, and at two o'clock on New Year's morning a hansom cabman called Hayman was summoned at the corner of Sidney Street and told to drive to the Shakespeare Theatre, Clapham. He took them – according to his statement and Muir's belief in it – to the corner of Lavender Gardens, where Morrison paid him five shillings. The distance was some six miles, and it had been discovered, by trial, that late at night the journey would take about thirty-eight minutes.

Here it may be noted that Hayman was one of three cabmen called for the prosecution, and during the trial there were occasions when they seem to have become evidence, not so much for the truth of what they claimed to have seen and remembered, as for the awful veracity of Shakespeare's genius when he put upon the stage those clowns whose speech and antics no longer seem quite so funny as, in their first incarnation, they must have been. The cabmen called for the Crown may not have been lineal descendants of Dogberry, but in their Cockney voices there was an echo of 'If you meet a thief, you may suspect him, by virtue of your office, to be no true man.'

If timings were correct, Hayman's cab reached Lavender Gardens at 2.38 a.m. To walk from there to the spot where the body was found – if the walkers did not pause to argue on the way – would take ten minutes. So Morrison was presumed to have begun his bloody work at 2.48 a.m. From the place of murder to a cab-rank at Clapham Cross was a walk of eleven minutes, and the second cabman, Stephens by name, had identified the prisoner as a man who approached the cab-rank, from the appropriate direction, between ten minutes and a quarter past three. Stephens drove his nocturnal fare to the Hanover Arms, near Kennington Church, where his passenger left him to cross the road in the direction of Kennington Gate. Stephens, thoughtful of his horse, walked it back to the Elephant and Castle, where he arrived at 3.40.

The prisoner had had about a quarter of an hour in which to murder, rob and mutilate his victim; and from the Hanover Arms it was only a few minutes' walk to a taxicab-rank beside Kennington Church. There the third Shakespearian cabman, called Castlin, had accepted a fare who, accompanied by another man, had called his taxi to drive them to Finsbury Park; and Castlin had subsequently identified Morrison as the man who engaged him. No attempt was made to identify Morrison's companion, or to explain his presence.

But the whole exercise, said Muir, had been carefully planned, from the wrapping-up of an iron bar in a parcel, to protracted loitering in the East End – a purposive delay to let New Year revellers leave the dark wind-blown waste of Clapham Common? – and so to Morrison's strange meeting with an accomplice who, on the assumption of a premeditated robbery, could only have been a receiver of stolen goods waiting to pay the murderer a meagre price for Beron's gold watch and chain. But are receivers of stolen goods so greedy for their profit that they take the risk of going to meet their purveyors? Purveyors hotfoot and red-handed? It seems unlikely.

Muir, however, was able to state the incontrovertible fact that Morrison knew Clapham Common well. For seven weeks, from the last week of September, he had worked for a baker, Mr Pithers, whose place of business at Lavender Hill was 'within a stone's throw' of where Hayman the cabman claimed to have put down his two passengers; and while in Mr Pithers' employment Morrison had delivered bread on a round that took him on to the Common.

There were witnesses, said Muir, who would swear they had seen Morrison and Beron together within an hour of the latter's death; and Hayman the cabman had identified Morrison as the man whom he had left, with Beron, at the corner of Lavender Gardens an estimated quarter of an hour before the act of murder. If the evidence of those witnesses was accepted, and his timing of events accurate, Muir had gone far towards proof of Morrison's guilt.

He then drew attention to the fact that Morrison, who was said to have been seen daily at the Warsaw Restaurant in company with Beron, was never seen there after his death except for a momentary visit on New Year's Day. For the next few days the newspapers had made much of the murder, but Morrison – so lately Beron's constant companion – never came to the restaurant to enquire about his death, and volunteered no information to the police. (In view of his criminal record, which was later made public, it would have been very strange if he had.) He did, however, go to the railway station of St Mary's, Whitechapel, and there deposited, under an assumed name, a parcel containing a revolver and forty cartridges. That was an act which could reasonably be explained by his fear of arrest while in possession of the weapon.

Two days before Christmas, presumably short of money, he had pawned a watch and chain for £4 10s; but on New Year's Day he bought a gold chain for £1 8s 7d, and in a paper bag he had a few sovereigns and at least two £5 notes. He cashed a cheque for £4 for Isaac Flitterman – father of dim-witted Eva – and gave Eva a present of £2. Where did that sudden wealth come from? The customers of the Warsaw Restaurant and their neighbours had fanciful ideas about money – that has been noted – and poverty inclined them to exaggerate the riches that lay in other hands and pockets; but Morrison himself admitted his comparative affluence in early January, yet could not account for it in such a way as to satisfy a sceptical enquirer.

Then Muir introduced a topic that was to provoke a great deal

55

of argument and anger until, at the trial's conclusion, Mr Justice Darling exposed its triviality. Soon after Morrison's arrest he offered to make a statement to Inspector Ward, who sent for Inspector Wensley. To Wensley the prisoner said, 'You have charged me with murder.' 'I have done nothing of the kind,' replied the Inspector. And at that time, said Muir, no charge of any sort had been preferred against the prisoner. From where, then, came his belief that he had been accused of murder? Out of his own, guilty, inner consciousness, suggested Muir.

A heated and inconclusive debate ensued about who said what – or who said it first – but eight days later the urbane Judge finally reduced it to its proper size and dismissed it as unimportant. Muir's stubborn pretence that Morrison suffered, at the time of his arrest, from a consciousness of guilt was otiose or irrelevant.

Muir concluded his case with a reference to blood-stains found on the prisoner's shirt and collar when he was arrested on 8 January, a week after Beron's death. They were very small, and looked like little spots of mud, but analysis had shown that they consisted of human blood. It was not explained why Morrison, who had plenty of clean linen in the room where he was living, should be wearing a week-old shirt; and Muir later admitted, by implication, the unimportance of the spotted cuff.

In a brief review of his case he reminded the jury of Morrison's companionship with the dead man; the pawning of his watch and his sudden affluence; his disappearance from the Warsaw Restaurant, or avoidance of it; his silence after the murder; and made the dubious assertion that on the night of the murder his movements had been traced for all but one half-hour, and during that half-hour Beron had been killed. Prudently he admitted that his case did not depend merely on a blood-stained shirt.

FIVE

R. D. Muir, counsel for the Crown

I

FIRST of the witnesses for the prosecution were police constables who offered a description of Clapham Common, the finding there of a murdered man and a plan of Gardner's Corner, in White-chapel, and the nearby streets. On the left of the map, at 32 Osborn Street, the Warsaw Restaurant was marked; on the right was Jubilee Street, where Beron had lived at number 133; next to it was Sidney Street, and leading out of Sidney Street was Newark Street, where Morrison had lodged at number 91. The customers of the Warsaw had lived in a slum-village where everyone knew everyone else and spoke Yiddish or Russian or French more easily than English.

The body of Leon Beron, lying among bushes a little way from an asphalt path that crossed the Common, had been dragged off the path – near which, apparently, the mortal blows had been struck – and tidily disposed in a less conspicuous place. No

C

attempt, however, had been made to conceal it. It lay on its back, its legs were crossed and the red-striped, black muffler that partially covered its head appeared to have been deliberately folded so as to cover the sides of the head and face, but to leave the front of the face, mud-stained and bloody, exposed. The head lay on the astrakhan collar of the man's coat, and the oddly formal appearance he presented had obviously made some impression on the mind of Constable Mumford, who discovered him. Mumford, at first sight, had thought that the wind-blown leaves, gathered under his coat-collar, were there to make a cushion for his head. But no one commented on the tidiness, the formality, with which the body had been laid upon its back; though its posture – a photograph records it – was certainly unusual for a victim of murder and robbery. If robbery had been the only motive, the murderer's departure would surely have been hurried. But seemingly he – or they – had lingered on the scene of the crime for several minutes.

It is not unduly fanciful to see, in the posture of the body, a deliberate exhibition of it. Under their mask of blood the cheeks had been scored with symmetrical cuts which, to early observers, had looked like a loosely drawn letter S; the head was hooded with the red-and-black muffler, but the face was uncovered; and the right leg had been laid neatly over the other. Was the body displayed for mockery?

A minor puzzle was created by Beron's hat, which lay at some distance from the body. It was described as 'unbroken', and presumably was a hard felt bowler or billycock. But if it was un-broken Beron must have taken it off, or the murderer removed it, before the fatal blows were struck. No attempt was made to solve that puzzle.

Abinger closely questioned a detective about photographs that showed the mysterious cuts on Beron's face. The photographs were copies of an original, and Abinger's purpose was to eliminate the possibility of their having been touched up. Mr Justice Darling could not see the point of his questions, and Abinger with apparent reluctance – as if he were not yet ready to reveal his motive – replied that it would be part of the defence to suggest that murder had been done, not for robbery, but vengeance.

Following the police witnesses came Frederick Freyberger, a pathologist, who described in detail the lethal wounds, and those dealt after death. The murderer or murderers had used, in his opinion, 'a blunt metallic instrument' which, if it were not heavy, must have been used with great force; and the body wounds had been inflicted by a knife with a blade at least five inches long. The latter wounds had been made while the body lay on its back.

The symmetrical cuts on the face were not deep enough to 'cause serious mischief', and Freyberger, who had previously described them as resembling 'an open S-shaped cut', now said they looked something like that. To a question from Mr Justice Darling he replied, 'They do not come out well in the photographs'; and added that on the dead man's face they had been distinct. In one photograph *rigor mortis* distorted them; in another they were blurred by the relaxation of the muscles after the *rigor* had passed off.

In the stomach were the remnants of a meal, and a strong smell of alcohol. The meal, about two-thirds digested, had included bread and meat, and Freyberger thought Beron had died between three and four hours after eating it. Abinger tried hard to persuade him to make more definite statements about the process of digestion, and how long a cup of tea and a piece of cake would remain in the stomach – how long before more substantial food would be absorbed or eliminated – but Freyberger was properly cautious and would not commit himself.

Abinger then drew attention to the prisoner's height – Steinie Morrison stood six foot three – and a man so tall, he said, would have had to stoop or kneel to make the cuts on Beron's face; in such a position his clothes would surely have been stained by spurting blood? But Freyberger disagreed. After a man has been killed or knocked unconscious, he explained, the arterial blood loses its impulse and no longer spurts, but merely oozes.

Joseph Needham, divisional surgeon at Balham, followed Freyberger and agreed with the pathologist's evidence. But he, who had seen Beron's body lying among the bushes, was careful to say that it had not lain squarely on its back, but somewhat tilted to the left side. On the front of the coat was mud and blood, and the back

59

of the dead man's hands and the toes of his boots were muddy. He had, it was obvious, been dragged face down to his last resting-place among the bushes, before being turned over. Death, said Needham – having felt for remnant warmth in the body – had probably occurred some six hours before his examination: that is to say, about three o'clock in the morning.

Questioned about the cuts on Beron's face, Needham agreed that he had recognised their resemblance to the letter S, but added: 'I think I described them as being like the "f" holes of a violin, on each side of the strings.' He was emphatic that they could not have been produced accidentally, and when Mr Justice Darling asked if they could have been caused by some roughness of the ground when the body, face down, was being dragged into the bushes, he said that was impossible: for the nose would have shown signs of such contact, and the nose was uninjured.

The cuts had been made with a knife, and Needham repeated what he had said in the Police Court: 'I thought it was extraordinary that anyone should have stopped to inflict such wounds.'

'Did you say', asked Abinger, 'that you thought they were some sign?'

'Yes. I said that at the Coroner's Court.'

A little clumsily, Abinger then tried to extract from him an admission that the cuts might represent the initial letter of the Russian or Polish word for a spy – or, more wildly, of some word of warning used by the Neapolitan Camorra – but Needham wisely replied that he knew nothing of such matters except what he had read in the papers.

His lordship, a sceptic, intervened: 'We must not have this.'

'I was asking,' said Abinger, 'because the witness said that he thought it was a sign, but I will not press it if your lordship thinks not.'

He returned to the processes of digestion, and the contents of Beron's stomach; but Needham was no more willing than Frey-berger to provide a precise and detailed timetable for the operation of gastric juices. Under re-examination by Muir, however, he said they had found in the dead man's stomach 'a mass' of partly digested food, which had not been closely inspected because they

60

had no microscope, but which could have been the remains of ham sandwiches; and as well as meat and bread there was 'a distinct odour of alcohol'. He also said that the murderer's principal weapon appeared to have been an angled iron bar – not cylindrical but sharp-sided – 'with a chisel-shaped extremity'.

II

These expert witnesses were followed by the dead man's brother Solomon; and with that sad figure there entered also an element of farce which the pathos of the scene could not disguise. For Solomon, acutely conscious of his dignity, was easily offended, and in his own ludicrous fashion proved a match, and perhaps more than a match, for Abinger, who pressed him hard – tried, as it were, to force him into a corner of the ring and keep him there – with, as it seems, two purposes in mind. Abinger wanted to expose the Berons' curious financial background, and to extract an admission that the habitués of the Warsaw, having discussed the evidence they would offer, were agreed that Leon's murder should be paid for by another victim.

Solomon was respectably dressed in a dark overcoat with a velvet collar, from within which rose a higher collar of starched linen. But his physical appearance was a little odd. A sadly drooping moustache overhung a firm lower lip, and above broad, flat cheekbones his heavily hooded eyes held a curious expression of bewilderment suffused with anger. His mental capacity was not large, but he could not be browbeaten into submission, and presumably he was slightly more intelligent than the other brother, David, who was not called.

He had, said Solomon, no occupation at all, and his dead brother, also without employment, had lived on the income of nine small houses, which brought him about £25 a year 'after paying all outgoings'. But Solomon's arithmetic is not to be trusted. Leon, he said, had no bank account, but carried his money in his pockets, and wore a gold watch and chain. At the time of the murder he had £12, and his watch and chain were worth about £30. Leon had been born in Russia, forty-eight years before, and when he was a year old the family removed to France, where they lived until 1894, when they came to London. He, Solomon, had last seen Leon alive at a quarter to eleven on Saturday, 31 December. He was standing on the pavement in Fieldgate Street, opposite the restaurant where Morrison was later arrested. He was alone, and when Solomon tried to speak to him he did not reply. On the following day Solomon identified his brother's body in the mortuary at Battersea.

He told Abinger that since Leon's death he and his brother David had been living at 133 Jubilee Street, where Leon had lived; and previously he had slept at Rowton House.

'That is a common lodging-house?'

'Yes.'

'At sixpence a night?'

With dignity Solomon replied, 'Three and six a week, and sevenpence a night.'

'Did you help your brother with the rent' – of the room in Jubilee Street – 'or did he help you?'

'My brother had nothing to help me.'

'Were you doing any work?'

'No.'

'What did you live on?' asked his lordship.

Solomon then explained that until a year before he had been living in Paris where he had worked for his sister as a *placier*, a traveller, selling drapery, and in London he had his savings to sustain him. He had come to London, he said, to make an application 'about some solicitors in regard to a trust estate'.

'Did it take twelve months to come over and make an application?'

Contemptuously Solomon replied – as if to rebuke Abinger for his ignorance of the law and its delays – 'There is a five years already my case is going on.'

Offensive in his turn, Abinger asked, 'Do you describe yourself as an independent gentleman?'

'Yes!'

'Living in a Rowton House at sixpence – I beg your pardon, sevenpence – a night?'

Then, with some justification, Solomon's anger exploded, and noisily he enquired, 'What is that to do with the case? It has nothing to do with the crime. If you ask me independent [?] questions, nothing relating with the crime, I will not answer you.'

Abinger continued to probe the strange monetary circumstances of the family, and Solomon said Leon had paid two shillings a week for the room in Jubilee Street, to which David, while living with him, had added ninepence. Abinger made play with the contrast between such penury and the considerable wealth that Leon had always carried on his person – wealth to which all the habitués of the Warsaw were prepared to testify – and with a barely controlled fury, that still one can almost hear, Solomon explained, as one of the elementary facts of life: 'Jewish people like jewellery! They buy jewellery to save money, as you always get it back again.'

His father, he said, was living in a Jewish home at 105 Nightingale Lane, Wandsworth. That was south of Clapham Common, but Leon, so far from showing filial affection, was not on friendly terms with his father, and had never gone to see him. He would swear to that. 'If you disbelieve me,' he added, 'I shall bring my father.'

Something in Abinger's manner again provoked his anger. Abinger may have shown, too openly, his disbelief; apparently he laughed. For Solomon shouted at him, 'It is nothing to laugh at! It is not a laughing matter. I do not see the joke. There is no joke in here to laugh.'

His evidence grew slightly incoherent, for when Abinger asked him at what time he had gone to bed on New Year's Eve he replied, 'When I go to bed was before I met my brother. I go usually this time.' He then corrected himself, but imperfectly, and said he had gone to bed at 10.45. From Fieldgate Street, where he had last seen his brother at 10.45, to Rowton House was 'five hundred yards, or three-quarters of a mile: that is all'. And he had gone straight to bed.

He could give no information, he said, about the way in which his brother used to spend his evenings. Nor did he know anything about the Anarchist Club in Jubilee Street. He knew there was an Anarchist Club – it was on the same side of the street as the house where his brother had lived – but he had never been there and could say nothing about it.

63

He admitted, again, that he did not work, and when Abinger, now offensively probing, said, 'You look very nicely dressed, and comfortable. Where did those clothes come from?' – the response was a cry of rage: 'Very well! Do you want to know?'

'I am dying to know,' said Abinger.

'I am not going to tell you. If the Judge asks me, I am going to tell him.'

There followed a rapid cross-fire of question and answer: questions designed to expose the financial shifts or shiftlessness of the mysterious Berons, to reveal the closed society of the Warsaw Restaurant; and answers that confused the issue by sheer stupidity, genuine misunderstanding or uncontrolled temper.

Mr Justice Darling told Solomon to answer Abinger's question about his suspiciously good clothes, and Solomon replied, 'You may tell him that I brought over in London about £100, money what I have saved from what I have made in Paris from my business.'

'Where is it?' asked Abinger.

'In the Bank of England.'

'You mean you have spent it?'

'Spent it, yes.'

'Have you got any of it left now?'

'I don't know that. I shall have a look.'

'At any rate, the jury are to understand that you are living in London, and you do no work?'

'Well, I get some property in London. I have got an estate.'

'What, Rowton Buildings?'

'If my lord would allow my application, I have got an estate. I will prove it to you that I have got an estate.'

'What does David do?'

'Nothing. He is doing some little jobs.'

'What do you mean by "little jobs"?'

'A jeweller.'

'Do you know a man called Fritz Svaars?'

'I do not know.'

'Do you know a man called Peter the Painter?'

'I do not know. No.'

'Have you ever met either of these men? Do you remember that you visited the restaurant of Mr Snelwar?'

'Yes.'

'Did you see a photo of Peter the Painter?'

'No. Mr Hermilin [a later witness] will say yes, that you showed a photo, and you have said that the prisoner, the accused man, is perhaps Peter the Painter. You have said that. Is that correct or not?'

His lordship intervened: 'You must not ask learned counsel questions. Just answer his questions.'

'Why should not I ask him questions?'

'You must not ask him questions because you are a witness, and he is not. That is the reason,' said his lordship.

'Will you swear', asked Abinger, 'that you did not know either of these men?'

'I do not know.'

'Do you know a boy named Rosen?'

'Do you mean the one who has been a witness in the case? Yes, since he has mixed in the affair.'

'Did you speak to Rosen after he had given evidence at the Police Court?'

'Never.'

'Now, listen. Did you say to Rosen if he came to Court and told the truth he would go to prison?'

'No, never.'

'And that he would be poisoned, or drowned?'

'I never spoke to him.'

'Do you know a boy called Jack Taw?'

'Only by sight.'

'Have you spoken to him since you gave evidence at the Police Court?'

'Never.'

'Have you seen Jack Taw in the Warsaw Restaurant?' (Jack Taw had briefly been a waiter there.)

'I do not take any interest in it. It has nothing to do with me in this case. If you take any interest, I do not. Do not put me so many questions or I will go out from here.'

'How many hours each day do you pass at Snelwar's restaurant?'

'I spend all the time what I got.'

'What time do you get there?'

'About one o'clock I goes, and I come in. I do not spend all the time there. Oh, it is no good talking.'

'Where else do you spend your time?'

'I go nowhere else, only to do my business.'

'What business?'

'I go to my solicitors. I cannot see the joke, what are you laughing at?'

'When did you go to your solicitors last?'

'Well, it was Friday, I believe.'

'Unless you are round at the solicitors you are in Snelwar's restaurant?'

'Yes.'

'Have you seen Mrs Deitch there?'

'I have.'

Mrs Deitch was soon to suffer grave embarrassment in Court, but it was not yet her turn to give evidence. Solomon was at last allowed to go, and following him into the witness-box came Alexander Snelwar, proprietor of the Warsaw Restaurant, whose evidence, under Muir's examination, appeared to incriminate the prisoner beyond hope of rescue.

Leon Beron had been his customer for six years, said Snelwar, and to other habitués of the restaurant was known as 'the land-lord'. He always carried a large sum of money, £20 or £30, in a wash-leather purse fastened by a safety-pin to his greatcoat pocket. Snelwar said he had known Steinie Morrison for about two months; he had been a regular customer since the beginning of November, and for the last three weeks of the year he had spent part of every day – half an hour or an hour – with Leon Beron. Morrison dressed well, and during their brief acquaintance had worn two or three different suits.

On 31 December Morrison was sitting with Beron at nine o'clock in the evening, and they remained together till a quarter to twelve. That, however, was a statement which Muir could not accept; for it contradicted Solomon's evidence of having seen his brother in Fieldgate Street at a quarter to eleven.

66

'Were they in the restaurant all that time, or in and out?' he asked; and Snelwar admitted that he could not remember. He repeated, however, that he had seen them at a quarter to twelve, and they had gone out together. Beron was wearing his 'big 18-carat gold watch, with a big chain and a £5 piece', and that was the last time Snelwar had seen him alive. But he had seen the prisoner again. On Sunday morning, between eleven and twelve, he said, Steinie Morrison had 'walked into the midst of the shop, and then walked out again, speaking to nobody'. But after that he did not return.

Cross-examined by Abinger, Snelwar said that Leon Beron used to arrive at the Warsaw at two o'clock, and remain there till midnight. He came every day, and all the year round.

'What would he be doing during those ten hours?' asked Abinger.

'Well, he was sitting and talking and eating all the time.'

But his meals were frugal, and his daily expenditure varied only between 1s 3d and 1s 6d. For supper on the thirty-first he had drunk a glass of tea at half-past nine, and that was all. He smoked a pipe, but sparingly. He spoke French or Yiddish. For ten hours a day, for five or six years, Leon Beron had passed his empty life at thinly spread tables in no activity except conversation. He had never worked, said Snelwar.

'Do you know', asked Abinger, 'that his income was about ten shillings a week?'

'I know he had nine houses. I do not know his income.'

'Do you know that his brother Solomon was living at Rowton House at sixpence or sevenpence a night?'

Snelwar knew that to be so, and Solomon's habit was the same as his brother's. He too sat in the restaurant for about ten hours a day, but came and left earlier.

His lordship asked Snelwar if his customers did any business while they sat together. But no, said Snelwar, they only came in to eat. That they did not eat much had been made pretty clear, and with splendid simplicity or commendable loyalty to customers whose daily lives were perhaps less innocent than he pretended he explained, 'They cannot afford to spend any more. I cannot make them go out of the shop if they have not got any money to spend.'

He was asked about a waiter called Jack Taw, soon to be called as a witness, and Snelwar said that Jack Taw, a boy of seventeen or so, was no longer in regular employment, but occasionally he gave him odd jobs to do. He admitted, however, that recently both Jack Taw and Solomon Beron had been in the restaurant every day. Then, deliberately, Abinger did what he could to discredit in advance another of the prosecution's witnesses, called Joe Mintz. The unhappy Mintz, also a waiter, had tried to hang himself in the restaurant. After which, said Snelwar, 'They took him away to Colney Hatch. He came out about three months ago.'

There were others about whom Abinger enquired – customers and prospective witnesses – and he suggested that Solomon, Jack Taw and two men called Weissberg and Zaltzman had, since the case against Morrison opened, been in the habit of sitting together to discuss it. Snelwar said that Solomon used to talk with Weissberg and Zaltzman, never with Jack Taw; but he was growing tired and beginning to contradict himself.

He said that Morrison had no money, and a few minutes later that he had often known him to carry gold. He denied having seen Morrison with a revolver, and promptly added, 'But I have seen him put it in his hip-pocket when he went out.' He said that all his customers had been talking about the murder of the three constables in Houndsditch. All, that is, except Leon Beron. 'I swear I never heard Beron talking about it.'

Abinger asked how, if Beron's income had been ten shillings a week, and his expenditure the same, he had been able to accumulate the £20 or £30 he was said to carry in his pocket. And Snelwar raised the financial mystery to new heights by replying, 'I hear that Beron brought from France £26,000, and he lost it here.'

That passed without comment, and when asked if he had ever seen Beron with women Snelwar replied emphatically, and probably with more truth, 'Never.' He clarified, for Mr Justice Darling, an earlier reference to a small business transaction with the prisoner – he had never bought a watch from Morrison, but

68

after Morrison had pawned the watch for thirteen shillings he had bought the pawn-ticket for half-a-crown – and the first day's proceedings came to an end when his lordship asked the members of the jury if they would like to visit Clapham Common. The Foreman said they would, and a brake was provided for them.

SIX

Edward Abinger, counsel for the accused

ON the second day of the trial the first witness was the unhappy Joe Mintz, and Abinger's encounter with him was almost as unfortunate. To Abinger it may have seemed that none of the prosecution's witnesses – other than those who gave formal or expert evidence – was worthy of much respect, and most of their testimony lacked substance. They were illiterate, stupid, biased, unreliable; and for one reason or another the stories they told were suspect from the start. If that was his opinion – and he had some grounds for it – his course of action was clear. He would defend his client by attacking and discrediting the witnesses called for the Crown. His attack was bold, but led him into danger. His manner, at times, was rough, and perhaps too rough; he may, by the ardour of his advocacy, have antagonised the jury.

During his examination by Muir, Joe Mintz behaved with propriety and answered questions with some assurance. He appeared to know what he was talking about. He had been a waiter at the Warsaw for two years, he said, and for all that time Leon Beron had been a regular customer. Steinie Morrison had been a customer throughout December, and for about a week before the crime – he corrected himself, and said for two weeks – he had been 'very good friends with Beron'; more friendly with him than with anyone else in the restaurant.

On 31 December Morrison came in about six o'clock, and to Mintz at the counter gave a parcel wrapped in brown paper, about two feet long, and four or five inches in circumference. 'Keep it for me,' said Morrison, 'and when I go out I will take it from you.' Snelwar's little daughter was standing near them, and asked, 'What is it?' Morrison told her it was a flute. He then joined Beron at his table, and for the whole evening, said Mintz, they sat together: only the two of them. Between eight and nine Morrison called for two glasses of tea with lemon, and after that Mintz served them nothing till about twenty minutes to twelve, when Morrison had a glass of lemonade.

On their way out, while Leon Beron stood beside him, he asked for his parcel. It was much too heavy for a flute, it felt like a bar of iron. Morrison did, in fact, own a flute, but when Mintz was shown it he said that was not what was in the parcel.

He appeared to lose some confidence when Abinger began to cross-examine, and contradicted himself when asked about who talked to whom, and which of the customers were on friendly terms. 'There are so many customers in the restaurant. They are talking together, but I do not know if they are talking about business, or friendly.' In this matter, it seems, Mintz was more realistic than Snelwar, his master, who was sure that his customers never talked business.

Then Abinger reminded the luckless waiter of his attempted suicide, and to his question, 'Did you try to hang yourself in this restaurant?' Mintz, with some justification, replied, 'I believe it has nothing to do with this case.'

'Is it true?'

'It is true, but it has got nothing to do with the case.'

Now Abinger wanted to know if, since his release from

Colney Hatch Asylum, he had made another attempt to hang himself.

'I do not tell you this,' said Mintz. 'That is my business.'

'I am sorry to have to ask you – '

'Very well, I am sorry you ask me. It has nothing to do with this case.'

At this juncture Abinger appeared to be walking blindfold into a legal trap which, with the best of intentions, had been constructed and set by the Criminal Evidence Act of 1898. That Act allowed a prisoner to give evidence on his own behalf, but made him subject to cross-examination. Under earlier rules a prisoner's past life had been his own secret; though he were guilty of a dozen previous crimes, no mention of them was permitted during the course of the trial. But now, if the defending counsel were to attack any one of the prosecution's witnesses on the ground of criminal, evil or untrustworthy character, then the prisoner would become equally liable to exposure; and such exposure could be dangerous to a man like Morrison who, more than once, had been in prison. Abinger's strategy depended largely on his ability to discredit the Crown's witnesses, but if he assailed their character he would offer Morrison as a reciprocal target for Muir's marksmanship.

To Mr Justice Darling it seemed that Abinger was unaware of the danger he invited, and he warned him of it: 'I suppose you realise, Mr Abinger, that suicide is a felony, and that you are asking this man if he attempted a felony?'

Abinger agreed, but clumsily tried to excuse his question by suggesting that, as Mintz had not succeeded in killing himself, he could not be held guilty of a felony: 'I am not imputing an offence to the witness at all. A man may be *non compos mentis* when he attempts to commit suicide.' And again he asked the wretched waiter, 'Have you more than once attempted to kill yourself?'

'Only once,' said Mintz, and answered Abinger's other questions without ill-will, without faltering; or so it seems from the record. He admitted a slight dispute with Steinie Morrison – the result of tardiness in serving his breakfast – and spoke of seeing Morrison and Beron together on the last night of the year.

They might have gone out 'for a few moments', without his noticing, but apart from that possibility they sat, for several hours, at the same table, and had no conversation with anyone else.

He enlarged the episode of the brown paper parcel, and put a little sentimental decoration on it. Snelwar's daughter Becky, who had asked what was in the parcel, was very friendly with Morrison, he said: 'He took too much notice of her every day.'

'How old is Becky?'

'Ten years.'

'Did he make a pet of her?'

'He used to play with her.'

Abinger left it at that, and Mintz reaffirmed the interesting fact that, after his midday meal of soup and meat, Beron had had nothing more to eat or drink than a glass of tea.

His lordship, remembering what the pathologist had said about the contents of the dead man's stomach, asked, 'Do you sell spirits, or beer, or wine?'

'No,' said Mintz, and added later that it had never been a practice of the restaurant to send out for drink, and he had never seen Beron take wine or spirits.

Watches and chains were a topic of permanent interest, but Mintz refused to identify a gold chain that Morrison was said to have worn since the end of November – his pawning of a silver watch had been, presumably, a convenient way of getting some small change – though he did remember that attached to the chain had been a half-sovereign. The parcel, about which little Becky had been inquisitive, made another appearance, and Mintz stoutly declared that it had held something longer and heavier than a flute.

He was allowed to go, and his place was taken by Henry Hermilin, a furrier who lodged above the restaurant and was another regular customer. He testified to the weight and value of Beron's gold watch – it weighed six ounces, three ounces for the movement and three for the case – and said that eight days before Christmas he had seen the prisoner take it from Beron, and heard him say, 'It is a very heavy watch.' On the night of the thirty-first he had seen them together, and they had gone out 'a couple of times, and then come back'.

Under cross-examination he faltered, and Abinger disclosed several discrepancies between his statement in the Police Court and the evidence he was now giving. But Hermilin knew more about gold watches than about the English language. Abinger, disputing his claim that Morrison and Beron had been on friendly terms for two weeks, reminded him that he had previously said he had seen them 'a couple of times talking together'; but, when Muir asked what he meant by a couple of times, Hermilin answered, 'It can be ten times, it can be more.' And to Mr Justice Darling's enquiry he reasserted that Morrison and Beron had been 'very friendly'.

Jack Taw, a boy of sixteen – 'going to be seventeen in a few weeks' – was casually employed by Snelwar. During the week after Christmas he had served in the restaurant, and he gave evidence that: 'On the evening of the last Saturday in December I left there at eight o'clock, and I went back at eleven. Leon Beron was in the restaurant when I went out at eight. The accused was with him, and they were sitting at the same table. When I came back at eleven they were still there. They went away together at 11.45.'

'Did you', asked Muir, 'see any more of them that night?'

'I saw them at a quarter to two at night, at the coffee-stall in Whitechapel Road, at the corner of Church Lane. They were on the opposite side of the road to me, and were walking along towards Mile End.'

'Have you ever seen the accused with a pistol in the restaurant?'

'Yes, he showed me a black pistol in December. He did not say anything when he showed it to me. He just took it out of his hip-pocket and showed it to me, and then he put it back again.'

Cross-examined by Abinger, he said he had been in England for three years, having come alone, as a boy of thirteen, from his home in Galicia. He had no father, and where his mother was he did not know. For a whole week's work Snelwar paid him seven shillings, but only once in two years had he been so continuously employed. For a day's work Snelwar would give him 1s 6d 'and eating'. He could not read, he did not know the months of the year; but he could tell the time of day.

That poor waif of the streets was tough, however, and had an appetite for enjoyment. During the morning of the thirty-first he had worked in the restaurant, and in the evening he went to 'a picture show' at the Cambridge Music Hall. At eleven o'clock he returned to the restaurant to draw sixpence, his pay for a morning's work, which would give him enough for a night's lodging. But he wasn't tired, he said, and not yet ready for bed. Someone was playing a piano in McCarthy's lodging-house in Brick Lane – a continuation of Osborn Street – and there, or on the pavements between McCarthy's and the coffee-stall from which he had seen Morrison and Beron, he had loitered, with other boys, till nearly two o'clock.

He was less assured when questioned about his association with Rosen, a boy who had sworn to having seen Morrison on the street at half-past one, and then admitted his mistake. He had spoken to Rosen during the Police Court proceedings, he said, but not 'about the case'; and he could not remember if Solomon Beron was present at the time. He had, however, taken Rosen to the police station, to offer his statement, and that was on the day of the battle in Sidney Street, at which he had been present. He denied having threatened or tried to influence Rosen.

Mr Justice Darling showed a wondering, indeed a protective interest in Jack Taw. It was his lordship who wanted to know if he had been in Sidney Street while 'the firing was on', and the soldiers fired in reply; and undoubtedly there was pride in Jack Taw's voice when he answered 'Yes'. And his lordship asked – as Abinger had asked before him – 'When you came over from Austria, did you come all by yourself?'

Again Jack Taw answered, 'Yes.'

'You came to get your living here?'

'Yes.'

'And have you been getting your living here ever since?'

'Very badly,' said poor Jack Taw.

II

There succeeded him in the witness-box Jacob Weissberg, a Russian butcher, and after him Israel Zaltzman, a Polish furrier, whose evidence, whether true or not – and certainly not all of it

75

was true – composed a nocturne of lugubrious farce. On the thirty-first, said Weissberg, he had seen Morrison and Beron together at half-past eleven in Commercial Street. His statement did not quite accord with the evidence of others who had been at the Warsaw, but as if to substantiate it he added, 'I was with my friend Mr Zaltzman at the time.' Later that night, at a quarter to one, he had seen them again – Zaltzman was still with him – in Whitechapel Road about fifty yards from the London Hospital.

When Abinger cross-examined, Weissberg said he had met Zaltzman, at the restaurant, about six o'clock, and for two hours they had walked to and fro between Whitechapel and the Bank. Between eight and half-past they had supped at the Warsaw, and then gone walking again, now between Aldgate and Mile End Road 'and then back again'.

'What time was it', asked Abinger, 'when you got back to Aldgate?'

'I cannot tell you exactly the time. Of course, we went there and back all the time.'

'You walked about all this time with Zaltzman?'

'Yes.'

'Were you getting rather weary? You had been walking about since six o'clock.'

One may imagine that here occurred a small, uncomfortable pause while Weissberg sought in his mind for some realistic detail with which to fortify his story. Invention came to his rescue, and he said, 'I also met a girl friend, and had a conversation with her.'

'The three of you walked about – you, the girl and Zaltzman?'

'Yes.'

'And so on, until a quarter to one in the morning?'

'Not with the girl. The girl left us about eleven.'

'Then did you go on walking backwards and forwards from Aldgate to Mile End?'

'Yes.'

'You would be getting very tired?'

'Yes, we got very tired,' said Weissberg.

When Zaltzman followed, he told a story substantially the same, but significantly different in detail. According to him, they

76

had begun their weary marathon at three or half-past three in the afternoon, in Whitechapel, Mile End Road and Shoreditch. It was half-past seven when they went to the Warsaw for their supper, and about eight o'clock they resumed their walk, between Aldgate and Mile End, and so continued till a quarter to one.

'Did you meet anybody?' asked Abinger.

'I met Morrison and Leon Beron.'

'Did you meet anybody besides Morrison and Leon Beron?'

'I have not seen any others.'

'Think carefully,' said Abinger, 'whether you did or did not meet somebody else, and walk with somebody else.'

Again there must have been a difficult pause while Zaltzman tried to remember what he had agreed to say; but memory played him false, and he answered, 'From the Mile End into Osborn Street somebody else also walked with us, but I do not know him by his name.'

Abinger took cold advantage, and asked, 'Anybody else besides that man?'

'Except this man,' said Zaltzman, 'nobody else spoke to us. I do not remember anybody else.'

Muir, re-examining, tried to cover the *gaffe* by asking, 'Did you have any conversation with any woman that night?' But Abinger objected to a leading question, and his lordship sustained the objection.

Perhaps the whole of that implausible tale can be dismissed as the clumsiest of fictions; but it must be observed that Zaltzman, having heard of Beron's death on the morning of Monday, 2 January, went that day to the police and made a statement. Then, on 10 February, Weissberg was induced to corroborate his evidence, and excused his tardiness by saying he had thought one statement would be enough. If, then, the evidence of Weissberg and Zaltzman is discarded as a farrago of dull invention and deliberate perjury insufficiently rehearsed, their appearance in the witness-box must have a sinister explanation. Did Solomon Beron, as soon as he had heard of his brother's death, go to Zaltzman and bribe him to incriminate Morrison? Did Zaltzman consent, but later begin to fear that his unsubstantiated word would not be accepted? And did he then persuade his friend Weissberg to join

77

him on their imagined marathon, but fail to synthesise the tale they were to tell? That might account for a ludicrous interlude in the trial; and Weissberg, indeed, admitted that he had gone to the police station with his story because 'a gentleman came to me and told me I was wanted'.

The ludicrous interlude was followed by a scene in which anger was released and decorum flouted. She whose voice rose loudest – in response to deliberate provocation – was Nellie Deitch, wife of a gas-fitter who also kept a small bicycle-repairing shop in Commercial Road. She had known Leon Beron for about twelve years, and at some time after one o'clock in the morning of New Year's Day she and her husband, returning from a party at her father-in-law's house, had met Morrison and Beron. She had never seen Morrison before, but they looked at each other, and after she had 'made an observation' to her husband – apparently in surprise 'about Mr Beron being his friend' – Morrison turned to look at her again. On Monday evening, having heard of Beron's death, she went to a police station and made a statement.

At the Police Court she and Abinger had already discovered their antipathy, and quickly it flared again. Having asked her husband's trade, he rudely enquired, 'What are you?'

'What am I?' exclaimed Mrs Deitch. 'I am a woman, of course!'

'I can see that, but what is your occupation?'

'My occupation? That is a fine question to ask me! I am at home in the house – looking after my children – looking after my business. We have a gas-fitting shop, and I look after it while my husband does the work outside.'

There followed some seemingly irrelevant questions about her added responsibility for looking after bicycle repairs, but they led to Mrs Deitch's admission that 'before living at 401 Commercial Road I was living at 4 Jubilee Street till about twelve months ago. We left because we failed in business there.'

'No other reason?' asked Abinger.

'No other reason.'

Then he launched an attack which, quite clearly, became an attack on character. His cross-examination of Joe Mintz could

78

possibly be excused as equivocal, but there was no doubt at all about the purpose of the questions he put to Nellie Deitch. He made a beginning with the seemingly innocuous query, 'Do you know a woman called Lizzie Holmes?'

Mrs Deitch swore that she did not. Nor did she know women called Dolly Nevy and Lena Hall. She had had a servant called Lizzie – she always kept a servant – but no women called Holmes or Nevy or Hall had ever lived in her house. Abinger, however, suggested that Lizzie Holmes, a prostitute, had paid three shillings a week for a room in Nellie Deitch's house in Jubilee Street, and a further three shillings for every man who stayed a whole night with her, a shilling for customers more quickly satisfied.

'I never heard of such a thing!' exclaimed Mrs Deitch.

'Where', asked Abinger, 'did you get that fur from?'

'That is my business!'

'Tell us, please.'

Her voice rose – it must have risen – as furiously she answered, 'Why should I tell you? You do not think I am as foolish as that?' And then, in vicious counter-attack: 'My husband bought it, what he worked for. I do not ask where your wife got her fur from.'

Abinger was not to be deterred, and suggested that Lizzie Holmes had followed Mrs Deitch from Jubilee Street to Commercial Road, and – on at least one occasion – done very profitable business for them both, when Lizzie and a man had each paid five shillings for a room, and Lizzie got fifteen shillings for herself.

Mrs Deitch knew nothing about that, and Mr Justice Darling intervened to say that he expected to see both Lizzie Holmes and Mrs Deitch in court on the following morning.

Mrs Deitch then confirmed that she had known Leon Beron for twelve years, but disclaimed all knowledge of his father. Leon, she said, had never spoken of him, though it emerged that between Deitches and Berons there had been, at one time, a certain intimacy. Before the years of his widowhood, Leon and his wife had been lodgers in the house of Nellie Deitch's father-in-law. Since his wife's death she had never seen him 'with a lady'; neither he nor Solomon had ever been to her house in

Jubilee Street; and about their father Solomon had been as reticent as his dead brother.

In Mr Justice Darling there showed a little impatience – or perhaps mere curiosity – about Abinger's pursuit of old Beron. 'Would it trouble you', he asked, 'to indicate what is his importance?'

It had been suggested, said Abinger, that no one but Morrison, who knew his way about Clapham Common, would have thought of going there. But if Beron's father were living on the southern border of the Common, he too 'must have known' it, and might 'not unnaturally' have gone there on New Year's morning. When Abinger said that, he must have known that he was contradicting Solomon's repeated assertion that his brother, on bad terms with his father, had never gone to see him. Abinger, apparently, thought Solomon was lying, and Abinger may well have been right. According to Fletcher Moulton the three brothers had met daily at the appointed hour for family prayer, and it is hard to believe that men so united by habit and respect for tradition – if not by affection – had entirely cut themselves off from their father.

Continuing his cross-examination of Nellie Deitch, Abinger asked her if, when she met 'her old friend' in the early hours of Sunday, she had stopped to wish him a happy New Year; and that simple question again woke her anger.

'Do you mean that at that time of the morning we were going to stop and wish them a happy New Year?' she demanded. 'We were going home, and we met many friends, but we were not going to stop to talk to everybody. We never spoke to them. We just passed them.'

'Neither you nor your husband ever said a word to him?'

'No.'

She may still, of course, have been playing the part of a respectable woman – too respectable to stop and gossip on a dark street – but her pretence to have passed Beron without a word of greeting or recognition is hardly credible. If, in fact, she and her husband did meet Morrison and Beron, it seems likely that there was some interchange of a sort she had no wish to admit.

She was not quite sure of the exact time of their silent meeting, but need not be blamed for that. She and her husband had left the party at her father-in-law's house about a quarter past one, she said, and half an hour later they stopped for refreshment at a ham and beef shop in Commercial Road. Having satisfied their hunger, and bought something for the children, they left the shop, saw Morrison and Beron and 'got home past two'. At the Police Court she had said it was nearly a quarter to three when they got home; and she admitted that she might have made a mistake. She was now quite positive that it was 'about a quarter past two' when they met Beron and the prisoner. She was equally positive that she had not seen a photograph of Morrison before she identified him, on 9 January, at the police station in Leman Street; but some doubt remained about that.

Following Nellie Deitch came the first of the three cabmen, Edward Hayman. He told Muir that about two o'clock on Sunday morning he on his high hansom, returning from the People's Palace in Mile End Road, spoke to two men walking towards Bow, and asked if they wanted a cab. That was at the corner of Sidney Street. One of the men, who wore a black bowler hat and 'a long greyish striped overcoat', was the accused, whom at a later date he had 'picked out from a number of others'; his second passenger was about five feet five in height and wore dark clothes and a bowler. The accused told him, 'I want to go to Lavender Hill', and asked him 'How much?' 'I leave that to you,' said Hayman, and got the satisfactory response, 'Very well, then, five shillings.' He then drove them 'at an ordinary pace' to the Clapham Junction side of Lavender Gardens, where the accused paid him. It was on 17 January that he 'picked him out from a number of other men at the South-Western Police Court'.

Abinger asked him, 'You, I suppose, along with other Londoners, heard of this murder on New Year's Day?' And Hayman virtuously replied – as if the company he kept was too sedate to talk of murder – 'I didn't hear of it, I just read it. It was in all the papers, of course.'

'On 1 January,' said Abinger, 'you drove a man to within a very few yards, as you say, of the very spot where this murder was committed.'

'It was not very far from it.'

'When did you first go to the police station?'

'About a week afterwards. I think it was the ninth, if I am not mistaken. I wouldn't be sure whether it was the ninth or the tenth.'

There followed a long and somewhat confused argument as to whether, before going to the police, Hayman had or had not seen a description of Morrison in the *Evening News* on the ninth, or 'a full-sized portrait' of him in other papers on the tenth; and about his reasons for delaying so long in reporting the undoubted fact that, on the night of the murder, he had picked up two men in Mile End Road, and driven them to within easy distance of the place where one of them was killed. Hayman himself admitted that it was rarely one found a passenger in Mile End – he was there only because 'he had been at the People's Palace after taking a fare from the Bank' – and agreed that the murder was notoriously the talk of the town. Since the sixth there had been police notices posted in every cab-yard in London offering the reward of £1 to a cabman who, between midnight and six o'clock in the morning, had driven two men from the East End to Clapham Common. But Hayman had been very tired that week.

'I was driving night work, and I went home tired after doing my work.'

'There was a reward attached, and London was ringing with the crime, and yet you were too tired to go?'

'I went when I thought proper,' said Hayman.

'The papers', said Abinger, 'were full of the Clapham murder.'

'I might go a week without looking at a paper,' said Hayman, perhaps priding himself on his singularity. But he knew that by Monday the second 'it was in all the papers', and when pressed to give a reason for the tardiness of his report he repeated, 'I went when I thought proper.'

'When you thought proper?'

'Yes, when I had the time. I was driving a cab all night, and I used to go home and go to bed in the daytime.'

Abinger again asked if, for a week or more, he had never connected, in his mind, the fare he took up in Mile End with the murder with which 'the whole of London was ringing'; and Hayman, having found a suitable almost liturgical response, replied, 'I went when I thought proper.'

Abinger reminded him of the police notice posted on the sixth – which he must have seen – and asked why he had not gone then.

'Because I was not sure whether I was – ' Hayman hesitated, and without revealing what he had been unsure of went on to admit, 'To tell you the truth, I didn't want to have anything to do with the job at all.'

What, asked Abinger, had he been going to say? But Hayman replied, 'I tell you, I can't give any reason for not going.'

Not until the seventeenth was he asked to identify Morrison, and in the intervening seventeen days, suggested Abinger, he had picked up and driven about 170 fares, who might be expected to have confused if not obliterated his memory of a man he had seen on New Year's morning. But, of course, there had been photographs of Morrison in the papers, and, said Abinger, 'It would be very difficult to find a man in London who could not identify the accused after a portrait like that which appeared in the *Daily Mirror*.'

'I did not identify the man from the portrait,' said Hayman, implying an ability to dismiss from his mind all memory of the portrait.

'Could you have identified the other man?' asked Abinger.

'No,' said Hayman, honestly enough, 'because Morrison was the one who engaged and paid me. I only know he was a man of five feet five or six, and dressed in dark clothes.'

Little more emerged from cross-examination, and Muir's re-examination, except Hayman's estimate that forty or forty-five minutes would have been the time for driving from Sidney Street to Lavender Gardens.

The day concluded with the brief appearance of Nellie Deitch's husband, Samuel. He described himself as a plumber, and said that in the twelve years of their marriage they had lived in five different houses. On their way home from the party at his father's house he had seen nobody he knew. 'I certainly saw plenty of people, but, of course, I didn't take much notice of any.' Like his wife he cultivated, or could pretend to, a habit that was reserved or even aloof.

'Did you see the late Mr Beron?' asked Muir.

'No.'

His wife, walking beside him, had seen and recognised Beron, and she had been impressed by the fact that his companion, in a long overcoat, was very smartly dressed. Had Samuel Deitch been looking the other way, or – after twelve years of marriage – had he fallen into the habit of contradicting his wife on principle?

Said Mr Justice Darling, 'You must not tell me what she said, but I want to know if you remember your wife making an observation to you as you went along?'

'Yes, she did. That was after we passed the men.'

Abinger asked, 'Your wife made many observations to you while you were walking home?'

'She did not. She only made one. She said she would like to have some refreshments.'

His lordship enquired, 'Besides asking for refreshments, did she speak to you on the way home?'

'She only spoke to me of seeing Beron with a young friend.'

The jury may have listened in some confusion to Deitch's evidence, but they must have concluded that in her own home Mrs Deitch's natural loquacity was not encouraged.

SEVEN

THE third day of the trial began in vulgar dispute. Mr Justice Darling had said that he wanted to see in Court both Nellie Deitch and her suspect lodger, Lizzie Holmes. Abinger brought, in two instalments, not only Lizzie but four other prostitutes who claimed to have been given house-room by Mrs Deitch. She denied all knowledge of them, they shouted 'Liar!' at her, and she screamed 'Liar!' at them. The members of the jury may, in consequence, have discounted Mrs Deitch's credibility as a witness, but as her only addition to the case for the Crown was a somewhat loosely determined time at which she claimed to have seen Morrison and Beron the devaluation of her testimony cannot have subtracted much from a small contribution.

After her came the second cabman, who was Andrew Stephens. He seemed, to begin with, a precise and solemn man, much more intelligent than Hayman, but self-conscious and perhaps a little too well pleased with himself, despite ill-health and recurrent bronchitis. He too drove a hansom cab, and he told Muir that on the early morning of 1 January, on the rank at Clapham Cross, he had picked up a fare – a man 'walking round the palings from the Old Town, Clapham' – and driven him to Kennington, where he set him down opposite Kennington Church. He had had 'an opportunity of seeing what the man was like', and he was quite sure that he was Morrison. He had not gone to the police till the tenth, but he had a better excuse than Hayman for his apparent tardiness; and on the seventeenth he had identified Morrison at the South-Western Police Court.

When Abinger began to cross-examine, Stephens revealed a memory remarkable for its accuracy. On 31 December, he said, he came out between two and three in the afternoon, and got off his cab at half past six next morning, after a spell of about sixteen hours. He had four fares with his first horse, and perhaps eight with the second: about twelve or thirteen fares. He could not say exactly how much money he had earned, but he had nineteen shillings at the end of the day. His last fare, before picking up the accused, was from the Royal Hotel, Blackfriars, to Cedars Road, Clapham. That took about half an hour. The fare before that was from Leicester Square to Clovelly Mansions, Gray's Inn Road. He wasn't exactly sure when he got to the rank at Clapham Cross, but it was just before the last tram went to Tooting. He thought it was between half past one and two o'clock. He picked up the accused about an hour after the last tram had gone, but he couldn't tell the time exactly.

'I was on the ground,' he said, 'when the accused came up, and I put my rug round me to jump up on my cab. It wasn't cold that night. It was a beautiful night.'

On Sunday night he had heard of a murder committed on the Common, but despite the fact that he had picked up a fare in the near vicinity, at about the supposed time of the murder, he had not told the police because he had not associated the man he drove to Kennington with the sort of man who might be supposed capable of such rude violence. 'I did not think this man had anything to do with it at the time.'

'Why?' asked Abinger.

'Because the general appearance of this man when he came to me was like an actor or a professional man, and I thought he lived in the neighbourhood of Kennington Park. I didn't go to the police because I never thought of it. It never entered my mind.'

That carries conviction, and Morrison could indeed have been mistaken for 'an actor or a professional man': he was tall, of uncommonly distinguished appearance and at the Warsaw his new suits had attracted attention. But the very precision of Stephen's memory, in other respects, may cast doubt on his identification. A little while later he said that his fare was his own height of five feet ten, and Stephens was not on the high seat of his cab when he first spoke to his passenger, but on the ground

86

beside him. Now Morrison stood six feet three, and a difference of five inches is not easily overlooked.

Abinger suggested that Stephen's imagination – his imagination rather than his memory – had been stirred by a newspaper description of the man whom the police had charged with murder; and asked when he began to think of identifying his passenger with the wanted man.

'On the Monday morning, 9 January.'

'On 9 January this man stood in the dock in an open Police Court.'

'I read that in the *Daily Chronicle* of 10 January,' said Stephens.

'Do you pledge your oath that you had not seen the evening papers of the ninth?'

'Yes.'

'Were you not sufficiently interested in what took place on Clapham Common as to want to look at the paper?'

Loftily Stephens replied, 'I hardly ever buy a paper.'

'You know that admirable paper, the *Evening News*, of course?'

Now Stephens became pompous – but perhaps forgetful of his acquaintance with the *Daily Chronicle* – and proudly replied, 'I never buy it and never read it. I am a democrat. If I buy a paper it is usually the *Star*. I did not read the *Star* or any other paper that night.'

Ignoring the challenge to political debate, Abinger read from the *Evening News* of 9 January:

> Clapham murder arrest. Accused man at the Police Court. Tall, well dressed. The ordinary cases of the day had been disposed of by 3.25, and two minutes later the place of a man charged with cruelty to a horse was taken by a tall, well-dressed, clean-shaven man, the accused. With Detectives Ward and Hawkins the man walked to the little iron-railed dock in the centre of the gas-lit Court, and faced the magistrate with complete unconcern. Morrison wore a heavy overcoat of rough greenish cloth, dark trousers, and well-polished, fairly new boots. He looked like a person in fairly good circumstances.

But Stephens swore he had not read that description before going to the police, though he had seen it, and a photograph, at a later date before identifying Morrison; which clearly made identification easier.

Abinger then read the statement that Stephens had made to the police on 10 January, in which he said that it was 'just before half past two' when, on the cab-rank at Clapham Cross, the man identified as Morrison had engaged him to drive to Kennington. If that were true, however, it contradicted Hayman's evidence, who had testified that Morrison was in his cab, on their way to Lavender Gardens, at that time.

Stephens then explained that he had told the police he was unsure of the time, but 'it was about one hour after the last tram went'; which he had supposed to be at half-past one. Later, assailed by doubt, he went of his own volition to the tramway company, and learnt that the last tram had left at 1.58. He reported his mistake to the police, who then timed him over the whole journey that Morrison was alleged to have made – from Sidney Street to Lavender Gardens, from Clapham Cross to Kennington – after which Stephens calculated anew the hour at which he had picked up Morrison, and made it a quarter past three.

He may, of course, have been entirely honest, but the alteration was suspiciously apt. For about forty minutes, according to Hayman, the prisoner had been in his cab, and now Stephens allowed him an opportune half-hour in which to do whatever he had to do in the darkness of the Common. He rebuffed a suggestion that the police had prompted him to make a change so useful to the prosecution, and denied having discussed the problem with Hayman.

Muir, re-examining, may have won a little sympathy for him by eliciting the fact that for four days of the week before the ninth he had to stay at home because he was ill with bronchitis; but the earlier impression of him, as a precise and scrupulous witness, must have been badly blurred before he was allowed to leave. In his opening statement, moreover, Muir had confidently claimed that the prisoner's movements on the night of the murder 'had been traced for all but one half-hour'; but that half-hour was now defined on a time-table opportunely amended to suit his case, and his case was buttressed by two cabmen who had seen photographs of Morrison before they identified him.

Members of the jury were, very properly, mystified or upset by what they had heard. Stephens, though dutifully admitting his initial mistake, appeared confident of having corrected his error and discovered, by divination if not by a clock, the time – so suspiciously close to that which the prosecution required – at which he had picked up a 'fashionably dressed' man in a long coat; and the foreman of the jury asked leave to put some questions, which Mr Justice Darling allowed.

Stephens was asked if, when he amended his timetable, he acted 'entirely on your own doing, or was it suggested to you?' 'I went entirely on my own,' he said, 'and made enquiries myself, and when I found they were right I went and told the police what I had done.' 'Entirely on my own,' he repeated.

'Before going to the tramway company and the police,' he was asked, 'had you seen Hayman to talk to?' 'No,' he answered, 'I have not seen him during this case. I never spoke to him about this matter'; and added, very strangely, that although he had known Hayman for four or five years he had not known, until 17 January, that he was a cabman. To believe that is difficult indeed.

Detective Sergeant Cooper gave evidence as to taking a statement from Stephens that contributed little of which either side could take advantage, but compels a belated sympathy for a witness who, 'when he came to the police station, had a bad attack of bronchitis and could scarcely speak'. Then Abinger recalled Nellie Deitch and confronted her with three more women – Dolly Nevy, Lena Hall and Becky Blue – known to be prostitutes; and Mrs Deitch denied all knowledge of them. To the jury his lordship explained that Abinger's purpose was to impeach Mrs Deitch's credit as a witness, and said also that he could do no more than exhibit the women: he could not call them as witnesses to contradict Nellie's assertion of innocence because, in law, he was not allowed to do so. The prostitutes' parade cannot have done much to fortify the case for the defence.

II

The third of the cabmen, Alfred Castlin, drove a taxi cab. In the early morning of New Year's Day, at about half past three, he had picked up, he said, two men on the cab-rank near Kennington

D

Church, and driven them to Finsbury Gate. On 19 January, at Leman Street Police Station, he had identified Morrison as one of them: the other man was shorter and spoke in a foreign tongue, but Castlin took little note of him, though when Morrison – if Morrison it was – appeared to hesitate after being told that the fare would be seven shillings, it was the shorter man who 'pushed him into the cab'. At Finsbury Gate, in Seven Sisters Road, Morrison gave him three half-crowns, and Castlin remembered that he wore a long overcoat, 'a motor-shape fashioned coat', and perhaps – though he could not be sure – a cap. He was sure, however, or 'near enough', that it was within a few minutes of half past three when he picked up his fares. He had, he admitted, been working for fifteen and a half hours, but he did not feel tired.

Abinger, for some obscure reason, asked if he remembered 'the anarchist outrage in Seven Sisters Road, or in Tottenham, or about there?' 'Yes,' said Castlin, but could not tell how far Tottenham was from that part of Seven Sisters Road where he had dropped his fares: 'I know nothing about Tottenham,' he said proudly. 'I am a London cabman, not a suburban cabman.' On 3 January he had read in the *Evening News* that the police were looking for 'two Frenchmen' who had been missing since the discovery of a dead body on Clapham Common – Leon Beron was at first, or by some, thought to be a French Jew – and on the fourth he had told the police about his two passengers who, if not French, were certainly foreigners and therefore, in Mr Castlin's opinion, open to suspicion. There was nothing else, he admitted, that led him to associate them with the murder on the Common.

Following him came Thomas Pithers, a baker whose shop at Lavender Hill was about fifty yards from Lavender Gardens, and who, from late September till early November of the previous year, had employed Morrison, paying him twelve shillings a week and giving him board and lodging. During the last ten days of his employment Morrison went on a round which took him to roads opposite Clapham Common. Pithers had a young family, and told Abinger that Morrison had been very nice to them: very nice and very kind.

The prosecution then led evidence to prove that on 1 January Morrison had deposited, at St Mary's railway station, Whitechapel, a brown paper parcel in which were later found a towel, a revolver and a box of cartridges. A cheque was produced, and its history narrated: Abraham Stitcher, a second-hand clothes dealer – but later described as a tailor – gave it to Isaac Flitterman, who testified that in the kitchen of the Flittermans' house Morrison had changed it for him, giving him eight half-sovereigns that he took from a paper bag in which, said Isaac, there were several £5 notes; and to his sister Eva – of whom more will be told – Morrison then gave two sovereigns as a present. Then followed evidence of Morrison's arrest, at the restaurant in Fieldgate Street, by Detective Inspector Wensley and four other police officers. Wensley denied having charged him with murder or made any reference to Leon Beron, but said Morrison had offered to make a voluntary statement because he, the prisoner, understood that he was accused of a serious crime – of murder, in fact – and in his presence Morrison had dictated a statement to Inspector Ward.

Abinger, in cross-examination, led Wensley on a circuitous route from the Houndsditch murders to the search for Peter the Painter and the siege at Sidney Street; to the anarchist club in Jubilee Street, the house in that street where Leon Beron lived and the proximity of Jubilee Street and Sidney Street; to Nightingale Lane on the south side of Clapham Common, where Beron's father lived, and a police request for information from any cabman who, on the night of the murder, had picked up one or more passengers on or near that side of the Common. 'Can you tell us', asked Abinger, 'why the police directed the attention of drivers to that neighbourhood?' and Wensley bluntly answered, 'No.'

Abinger referred to a map of the Common, but seemed to lose his way – or lose sight of his immediate purpose – and his lordship showed a little impatience.

'What is the question?' he asked, and Abinger was unable to find a phrase to fit what he had in mind. He gave the lame reply, 'One has to be so careful in a case of this kind in forming one's question.' Then, changing the subject, he brought Wensley back to the matter and manner of Morrison's arrest, and Wensley again denied having said, 'Stein, I want you for murder.'

Now Abinger revealed a sudden firmness, and pressed Wensley hard. 'You did not arrest him on suspicion of having committed murder? Do you swear to that?'

'I do.'

Morrison had not been arrested until a week after Beron's death, and it cannot be doubted that there was scepticism in Abinger's voice when he asked if, by that time, the police had heard no statement nor received information connecting him with the murder. But again Wensley said, 'No.'

Mrs Deitch had made her statement on 2 January: that curious tale of meeting Morrison and Beron walking together when she and her husband were on their way home from a party. 'Did not that connect Morrison with the murder?' asked Abinger. 'Only by her description of him,' replied Wensley, less robustly than before.

And Castlin had made his statement on the fourth: 'After that did you not connect Morrison with the murder?'

'I did not connect him with it till he was identified,' said Wensley; and that must have put a strain on the Court's credulity.

Then Abinger showed him a copy of the *Daily Graphic* of 9 January, in which there was a photograph of the restaurant in Fieldgate Street, and asked, 'If you did not mention at that restaurant that you were arresting Morrison for murder, how could that photograph have got into the paper the next day?'

'I don't know,' said Wensley, and feebly added, 'It might have got there in different ways.' Wensley – in goal, as it were – had been beaten, and Abinger had scored.

Re-examined by Muir, Wensley said that he was the officer of the Metropolitan Police in charge of enquiries into the Houndsditch murders, and that information about them, available to the City Police, was equally available to him; and agreed that he had known Leon Beron for four or five years, or longer.

'So far as you know,' asked Muir, 'was Leon Beron in any way connected with the persons responsible for the Houndsditch murders?'

Abinger objected, then withdrew his objection; but when Muir repeated his question exclaimed, 'I have never suggested that he was.'

It was Abinger, however, who on that day had introduced the Houndsditch topic, and Muir persisted in dissociating Beron from it. Wensley agreed that informers had helped the police, but Beron, he said, was not one of them. Nor, he declared, had the date of the murders and the date of the siege in Sidney Street 'any connexion whatever' with the death of Beron.

As well as the anarchists in their club, and Leon Beron at number 133, Mrs Deitch also lived in Jubilee Street, and Wensley did what he could to re-establish her as a reputable witness – and erase the memory of Dolly Nevy, Lena Hall and Becky Blue – by testifying that numbers 4 and 5, the houses she occupied, had been respectably conducted. He knew also that Leon Beron's father lived in a Jewish Home for Incurables in Nightingale Lane, and when Mr Justice Darling asked about his acquaintance with Leon Beron replied, 'He apparently did nothing by way of occupation. He was chiefly in this Jewish restaurant in the East End, and he was reputed to be a fairly wealthy man.' To the police, he added, he was known 'only by sight'; but Wensley, one feels – Wensley who knew all that the City Police knew, and was an officer of outstanding ability – knew more than he admitted, though his knowledge may have been far from complete.

Detective Sergeant Brogden confirmed, or repeated, the evidence already given about Morrison's arrest on 8 January, and said he had searched him at the police station and found two Bank of England notes for £5, £4 in gold, 5s in silver, 6d 'in bronze', a lady's gold watch, latch key, comb, 'and several memos'. On the same day he went with Inspector Ward to 116 York Road – where Morrison had admitted to living for some time with a young woman – and there made the acquaintance of Florrie Dellow, and in her presence 'took possession of a quantity of man's wearing apparel from different parts of the room'. At midnight, in the police station at Leman Street, he and another officer stripped Morrison of his clothing, and 'found a small spot of blood on the collar and on the left side of the tie, and two small spots of blood on the left hand cuff of the shirt'. As Wensley had done, he swore that no charge of murder had been made, when Morrison was arrested, nor was there any reference to the death of Leon Beron. Two of the police officers who had been with Wensley made the same assertion, and two others declared that Morrison had told them he 'wanted to make a confession'.

Detective Inspector Alfred Ward, who at nine o'clock on 1 January had seen Beron's dead body on Clapham Common, told of finding in his pockets at the mortuary 'a halfpenny, a tobacco pouch with tobacco in it, a pair of gloves, two keys, a handkerchief, some pieces of black paper, and two paper bags, one of which contained some pieces of ham sandwich'. He had spoken to Solomon and David Beron, and a Detective Jones had taken from their father a statement that can have been of no interest or value, for no other reference was made to it. He had 'directed a watch to be kept on 91 Newark Street', and the accused was arrested, 'having been seen coming from that house, on the morning of 8 January'. In the afternoon, in the presence of Inspector Wensley, Morrison told him that he wanted to make a statement. 'He said "I understand I am detained here on a very serious charge, of murder, I am told, and I desire to make a voluntary statement."' The statement, duly made, was taken down, typewritten and signed by Morrison.

On the following day, after his clothes had been taken from him, Morrison asked the reason and Ward told him there were blood-stains on his shirt and collar. 'Not blood,' said Morrison, 'that's mud I got yesterday.' Whether mud or blood, it is quite improbable that Morrison, a man who had a sufficient wardrobe and took more than a little pride in his appearance, should have been wearing, a week after the crime, a shirt and collar stained with the blood he was alleged to have shed on the dark morning of New Year's Day. A man of dirty habit, of the most limited intelligence and too poor to own a spare shirt, might have been trapped by such evidence; but Morrison – supposing him to have been guilty – was still a man of considerable intelligence, respectful of cleanliness and possessed of a decent store of underclothes. There may well have been a spot or two of blood on his shirt, but assuredly it was not the blood of Leon Beron.

Ward also told of searching Florrie Dellow's room, with

94

Sergeant Brogden, and of taking from it a black bowler hat in the lining of which a ticket was found that enabled him to retrieve, from St Mary's railway station in Whitechapel, the brown-paper parcel containing a revolver and forty-four cartridges. With Sergeant Cooper he had followed the route that Morrison was said, by the prosecution, to have taken in the morning darkness of 1 January, and timed his journey: by hansom cab from the corner of Sidney Street to the corner of Lavender Gardens, thirty-eight minutes; walking with Cooper from Lavender Gardens to Clapham Common and the place where he had seen the dead body, ten minutes; and so on, till the times, added together, fitted neatly into that segment of the night in which, according to the official view, murder had been done and Morrison had been there to do it.

Before the Court adjourned Ward described his discovery, in a gladstone bag taken from Florrie Dellow's room, of a ticket dated 23 December 1910, for the pawning of a gold albert for £4 10s, by one Stanley Morris of 16 Sidney Street. But at 16 Sidney Street he had been unable to find 'any such person'.

EIGHT

TALK of ham sandwiches opened proceedings on the fourth day of the trial. Inspector Ward, cross-examined by Abinger, said that in one of the two paper bags found in Leon Beron's pockets there had been some small pieces of bread and ham. On the bag were the name and address, Wright & Son, Royal Standard Arrowroot Biscuits, 183 Commercial Road. It was the address of a refreshment shop, said Ward, selling 'ordinary refreshments, ginger beer'. Later in the day Sergeant Cooper, recalled by Muir, said he had gone to 183 Commercial Road and 'found it to be a pastry cook's shop where they sell various cakes. They do not sell sandwiches there.' If Abinger had hoped to throw light into the obscurity of those last hours before Beron was killed – if he had suggested that Beron had bought sandwiches in Commercial Road before going to Clapham Common – his hope was defeated and mystery still darkened the circumstances of that final meal which, on a pathologist's evidence, had included alcohol, in some form, as well as bread and ham.

Ward spoke also of finding Beron's bowler hat, undamaged, about four yards from the body, and testified that in the bushes where it lay there had been no sign of a struggle. Abinger tried to show that he had been negligent in failing to take evidence from a night-watchman whose hut was said to be within a couple of hundred yards of the scene of the murder; and then returned to the old topic of Morrison's arrest while he was at breakfast in Fieldgate Street. The voluntary statement he had made in the Leman Street police station was produced and read:

I have sent for Divisional Detective Ward and Wensley and desire to make a voluntary statement in consequence of my having been arrested this morning under the suspicion of murder – Mr Wensley having told me this. I am an Australian, born in Sydney, brought up in England. I am a confectioner and baker, and now a traveller in common jewellery. During the month of September I obtained a situation as a journeyman baker at 213 Lavender Hill. I should think I was there about ten weeks altogether. I was sleeping there during the whole of that time. I left of my own accord, having saved up about £4. I then commenced to travel in cheap jewellery. I went to reside at No. 5 Grove Street, E., and remained there for two weeks. I bought the cheap jewellery from various persons; you will find the receipt for some of it in my bag. On leaving Grove Street I went to reside at No. 91 Newark Street. I remained there until last Sunday the 1st, and then went to live with a girl named Florrie at 116 York Road, and have continued to live with her up till the present time. Last night I stayed with a friend named Mrs Cinnamon, who lives in a building off Grove Street – the number is 32, and is next to a grocer's shop – as I was too late to return to my lodgings. This is my voluntary statement and all I wish to say.

As a statement it is remarkable for what he did not say: he made no attempt to account for his movements on the last day of the Old Year and the first day of the New Year, except to say that he left his lodging in Newark Street and went to live with Florrie Dellow. And to the credit of the police it should be noted that he was allowed to say that he had been 'arrested under suspicion of murder – Mr Wensley having told me this'; though Wensley and other police officers had emphatically denied that.

Nine persons were alleged to have identified Morrison at the police station: Alfred Castlin, Thomas Green, Mrs Deitch, Snelwar, Hermilin, Taw, Rosen, and Monschein and Minnets. The last two survive only as names; they were not called and made no subsequent appearance. Then there were questions about a blood-stained handkerchief, found on the Common on 2 January about 600 yards from the scene of the murder, and given to the police by a Miss Saunders. According to Abinger it had on it a foreign laundry mark; but according to Inspector Ward it had nothing to do with the case because it was not found until twenty-four hours after discovery of the body of the murdered man. The police had tried, but in vain, to find the laundry whose mark it bore; and when Abinger said, 'I am going to ask you to assume for the moment that the man who committed the murder dropped that handkerchief, and that he wiped his hands on it' Ward coldly answered, 'I do not assume he dropped it there.'

Ward was no more helpful when Abinger spoke of the Long Pond on the Common, by which, if the murderer were on his way to Clapham Cross, he would have to pass. A convenient place, suggested Abinger, in which to get rid of the murderous weapon? Yes, said Ward, but it was dry at the time, except for about a yard of mud on the bottom, and that had been searched.

'Was anything found?' asked Abinger.

'No,' said Ward; and then, 'I ought to alter that answer. There have been several things found.'

'I mean relating to the case?'

'Oh,' said Ward, with splendid indifference, 'I can't tell you.' But later it was admitted that some iron bars had been retrieved from the muddy bottom of the pond.

There was question and answer about what had been found, belonging to Morrison, in Florrie Dellow's room; and it was established that his wardrobe was not so meagrely furnished that he would have to wear a blood-spotted shirt a week after the murder of which he was accused. He had, for example, gloves and two white silk handkerchiefs, six other handkerchiefs, ten linen collars and three pairs of white cotton pants. Later, after inconclusive discussion about the briar pipe found some forty yards away from the body of the murdered man – Snelwar, the proprietor of the Warsaw Restaurant, had sworn that Beron used to smoke a clay pipe – Ward admitted that he had gone to the Japanese Sanitary Laundry, off the Commercial Road, where Morrison used to send his washing – and which was, in fact, the property of a Russian Jew – and there paid eightpence for recovery of a shirt, two or three collars, two handkerchiefs, one or two pairs of socks, a sheet and a large bath-towel. Whatever the source of his income, it seems clear that Morrison spent a fair proportion of it on his clothes and personal cleanliness.

More conversation followed – 'conversation' is, I think, the descriptive word – about the pieces of iron found in the mud of the Long Pond, and Solomon Beron's identification of the briar pipe as belonging to his brother. Then Inspector Wensley was recalled, to be cross-examined by Abinger, and what ensued was evidence that contributed little or nothing to elucidation of the central mystery, but revealed much about the nature of the witnesses who had been summoned: about the habit of their thin-ribbed existence, and the miserable tenuity of their association with the robust and careless life of the metropolis to which they had fled for sanctuary. Wensley was questioned about that silly girl, Eva Flitterman, who had given evidence when Morrison was formally charged at Leman Street police station, and then retracted what might have been its vital element: she had had the honesty to admit that she had mistaken the value of the coin that Morrison wore on his watch-chain. She had made a long statement to the police, which now was produced in court; and Abinger read it.

Eva, aged eighteen, a tailoress and single, whose father had died a few weeks before, had, on 24 December, been introduced to Steinie Morrison by a man she knew as Issy. Steinie, she had said, was then wearing a lady's watch and a chain from which hung a gold sovereign. Dim-witted she may have been, but she was sustained – as one gladly discovers – by a resolute vanity and a determination to assert the virtuous habit of her life before inquisitors who may well have doubted the truth of what she told them. Steinie, she declared, had made her an offer of marriage, and she had rejected his advances until marriage should license them. There is no disputing the fact that Steinie – so tall and handsome, of such distinguished appearance in the drab street where he lived – was unhampered by bourgeois morality, took his fun where he found it and paid for it when necessary. But there may have been a little truth in what Eva said. It is difficult to believe in the offer of marriage, but perhaps she had set a price on her virtue that convinced her of its value.

Towards the end of December she had met Steinie at the corner of Newark Street, and they had remained together – walking, as it appeared – from six in the evening until ten. Steinie had told her he was single and 'a jewellery traveller'. He offered to introduce her to his landlady, and two days later, on the twenty-eighth, she went with him to his ground-floor room at 91 Newark Street, where she remained for four hours. But during that time they were not left alone, she said, for his landlady and her two children kept coming in and out of the room. Steinie had shown her a brown paper parcel that concealed a flute, on which he played a few notes. At about eleven o'clock he walked home with her and, said Eva, asked 'Would you like to stop at my place with me all night?' She, pretending to think he was joking, replied with due propriety, 'If you marry me, then I will stay with you always. I am a respectable girl.'

On Sunday, New Year's Day, said Eva, 'he called at my house and told my mother that he would like to marry me'. Also there, in the kitchen where Steinie sat for three-quarters of an hour, were her brother and her married sister, and to them – if Eva can be believed – he showed the money he carried: gold, and what Eva thought were cheques, in a paper bag. And now, on his watch-chain, he wore a £5 gold piece which he said he had got from Paris. He gave Eva £2, and for her brother changed a cheque for £4, paying in half-sovereigns. At about 8 p.m. he left, and Eva walked with him to the corner of the street, where he told her that he had left his umbrella behind.

On Monday he called twice, inviting her the first time to go with him to a music-hall, but 'My mother won't let me,' she said. He returned in the evening, took off his overcoat and Eva saw that now the £5 gold piece had been removed from his watch-chain. 'Where is it?' she asked, and Steinie told her he had pawned it; but a few minutes later said he had exchanged it for a gold watch that he had left with the watchmaker. On Tuesday, 3 January, Steinie came back to look for his umbrella, and Eva's mother went to her workshop at 75 Commercial Street to get it, for Eva had been using it. They never made appointments, she said, but 'when I wanted him I went to 32 Osborn Street for him' – the Warsaw Restaurant, that is. Eva cannot have gone there very often, however, for Steinie gave up eating there after the murder. When he left her on Monday he promised to see her again on the following Sunday, 'but he never came', and a few days later she heard that he had been locked up.

Questioned again by the police on 24 January, Eva repeated in substance what she had previously told them, but admitted she had been frightened and confused when first interrogated. She insisted that she had never gone to bed with Steinie; said once more that he had asked her to marry him; and added the pleasing information that the tailor she worked for was called Mr Stitcher. She explained her reason for thinking that the gold coin she had once seen on Steinie's watch-chain was a £5 piece: her dead father had also worn a watch-chain from which hung a coin, and Eva had believed that to be a £5 piece. 'But I did not know what money was. I asked my mother what my father had on his chain. My mother said it was a £2 piece. When she told me that I went to the police station, Leman Street. I saw a fat man. He asked me to come at half-past nine. I then saw a man who is now in Court.' (She meant Wensley.) 'I told him I had made a mistake, he told me I should have to go somewhere else to tell them, and yesterday I went to the office of prisoner's solicitors and made a communication to them.' That Eva's faculty of observation was as limited as her memory was erratic must be admitted; for the coin on Steinie's watch-chain was – as later became known – a Kruger half-sovereign. But she was honest enough, and had sufficient sturdiness of mind, to admit her mistake.

Abinger appears to have been convinced that she had wilfully committed perjury, and applied for a warrant against her, presumably in the belief that further exposure of the unreliability of a witness for the prosecution would weaken Muir's case. The Director of Public Prosecutions refused his application, however, and there seems little doubt that Eva was guilty, not of malice against Morrison, but merely of ignorance. A suspicion remains, however, that the police had been a little too eager to assemble testimony against the accused, and had neglected to weigh the veracity – the validity of her memory – of their witness: if, on the day of the murder, Morrison had in fact been wearing a £5 or five-guinea piece he would have been advertising his guilt, for that was the very ornament which, in the Warsaw Restaurant, made the wealth of Leon Beron so conspicuous.

The other witness who had made statements that he later withdrew was Sam Rosen; his depositions were also produced and read by Abinger. Though no more than eighteen years old, Rosen, a Russian, had lived for two years in America, had been in London for only a couple of months and worked 'for anyone in a shop'. He had first given evidence on 24 January, and again, 'at the request of the prisoner's advisers', on 8 February. In his original statement he said he had known the prisoner for about five or six weeks, and 'knew he had a revolver in his pocket at the restaurant'. Morrison and Beron had left the restaurant at about half-past eleven, when Rosen also left, and later, at about half-past one, he saw them again in Brick Lane. For two hours he had been walking about with a friend, but he didn't know his friend's name. His friend, also a Russian, had recognised and greeted him.

When he was recalled Rosen said that on the night of 31 December he had slept at 28 Troshe Place, 'in Louis Mitchinsky's house. I slept in half a room, and Mitchinsky and his wife and child in the other half.' He couldn't remember when he came in, and though he had certainly seen the prisoner somewhere in the streets he couldn't swear to the time. After giving evidence at the police court he had had a conversation with Mitchinsky, who said he had been telling lies. Then he told Mitchinsky that he wanted to tell the truth, and Mitchinsky made arrangements for him to see Morrison's solicitors: 'I wanted to tell them the truth, which was not told to the police at the police station.'

He had been warned not to retract the evidence he had given: 'People have told me that what I have sworn I must keep to, and I must not put anything else in because I might get prison.' Beron's brother was one of those who told him that. But Rosen now denied having seen Morrison and Beron at half-past one – 'The actual time I did not know' – and contradicted his alleged statement that in the restaurant Morrison had carried a revolver: 'I did not tell Inspector Ward that I saw Morrison with a revolver, someone else said that, a man Jacobs, the lad who now stands up in Court. I did not say anything, it was Jacobs who spoke.'

It was, apparently, Jacobs who had first persuaded Rosen to go to the police and offer his evidence. He had come into the restaurant, where Rosen was still working, and asked if he wanted to look at some pictures – photographs of Morrison, presumably, that the newspapers had published. 'If you want to write your name in as a witness, you can,' said Jacobs. 'If not, it is nothing.' Rosen, when he swore to that, may have been speaking the truth, but not the whole truth; for surely Jacobs had some inducement to offer? Then, when Rosen changed his mind and wanted to withdraw his evidence, Jacobs and Samuel Deitch, as well as Solomon Beron, had warned him of the consequences, and others, whom he could not name, had threatened to shoot him.

Rosen may have suffered from an inflamed imagination as well as a guilty conscience. It was Jacobs, he said, who told him to swear he had seen a revolver in Morrison's hip-pocket, but 'before I came to Court today I did not tell Jacobs that if the prisoner was convicted I should be killed', or that Mitchinsky was one of those who had threatened him with death. Rosen's testimony was too incoherent to reveal much beyond a troubled conscience and continuing fear. What first induced him to give evidence for the prosecution remains obscure, and what persuaded him to retract it is also in doubt, though one cannot exclude the possibility that he did indeed want 'to tell the truth'. What, however, was Jacobs' interest, and what part, if any, was played by Rosen's Russian friend, with whom he walked the streets but whose name he could not remember? Rosen may well have been as nervous as he said he was when he gave his evidence in the Police Court, but someone or something had stifled his initial fear – perhaps with a greater fear.

The continued existence of Max Beron, father of the dead Leon and his brothers, was proved by Maurice Myers, secretary for a home for aged Jews in Nightingale Lane. The old man had been there since October 1908 – he was now very weak as well as old – and, though Solomon Beron had visited him, Leon, within Mr Myers' knowledge, had never gone to see him.

The case for the prosecution was nearing its end when Muir called Detective Constable John Jones, who had taken statements from the cabmen Castlin and Hayman, as well as one from Max Beron. Muir seems to have found no profit or advantage in what

Jones had to say, other than his corroboration of Myers' evidence, but Abinger took his opportunity to cross-examine and in the statements made by the cabmen found discrepancies that had already been noticed. Castlin had said that his suspect passenger stood five feet eight, but without hesitation had identified him as Morrison, whose height was six feet three; and Hayman, whose taller passenger was indeed a six-footer, had said he was wearing a black, hard felt hat; but in Castlin's cab the suspect wore a cap.

Muir called the last but one of his witnesses, Dr William Robert Smith, Professor of Forensic Medicine and Toxicology at King's College Medical School. His evidence was that on 10 January he had received from Inspector Ward a collar, a tie and a striped cotton shirt. On the collar were 'a number of spots'; on the tie three spots; and a sleeve and cuff of the shirt showed 'some marks'. The spots and the marks were subjected to analysis, and further examination revealed that they consisted of blood: 'Either human blood or the blood of higher apes,' added the Professor, gravely admitting that science had its limitations.

Abinger suggested that the spots on the collar – a tall, starched collar, size $15\frac{1}{2}$ inches by $2\frac{1}{2}$ inches – were no bigger than the head of a pin. 'They were very small,' admitted the Professor. 'About the same size as a spot of blood would be if a man scratched his neck in pinning his collar?' asked Abinger. 'There are a number of spots, two of which were in the form of streaks. I do not think a man could do that by scratching the back of his neck,' said the Professor. 'They were a quarter of an inch long.'

That, to Abinger, seemed the likely length of a mark left by a pin; and he turned his attention to the 'little tiny smear' on the cuff of the shirt-sleeve. He made Morrison put on his overcoat, and pointed out that the cuff of the coat-sleeve entirely concealed the shirt-cuff. It would be almost impossible, he suggested, for blood to have reached the base of the shirt-cuff when Morrison was wearing his coat. There was no suggestion that blood had been found on the coat, and the Professor admitted that it would have been 'very difficult' for the shirt to become smeared. Inside the coat-sleeve, moreover, there was an elastic band, a 'wind-protector', and with the wind-protector in position it would be a physical impossibility, said Abinger, without the elastic band also being stained.

'That is very difficult to say,' said the Professor.

'You are here as an expert?' asked Abinger.

The Professor admitted it, and Mr Justice Darling came to his rescue: 'While you call the witness an expert, he is not an expert in wind-protectors and cuffs. He is an expert in analysis, not in overcoats.'

Abinger accepted the rebuke, and the final witness for the prosecution was examined by Muir's junior, Mr Leycester. He was Dr Henry William Wilcox, senior scientific analyst to the Home Office. Between thirty and forty articles of clothing had been sent to him for analysis, but he had found no blood on any of them except the collar, the tie and the shirt.

To a question put by Mr Justice Darling he replied that when he gave evidence before the magistrate he had said he knew Dr Freyberger – the pathologist who made a post-mortem examination of Leon Beron – and agreed that if, as Freyberger had testified, 'there were six cuts on the right side of the face and three on the left, and three stabs on the body, and blows on the head, a considerable amount of blood would flow. I can quite believe that there would be a pool of blood on the ground where the deed was done, and a certain amount of bleeding would take place after death. Assuming that the deceased was dragged some distance along the path by the collar of his overcoat, I should not necessarily expect to find a great quantity of blood on the clothing of the person who did that. It would depend upon how it was done. It would be possible for a great deal of blood to get on his clothing, and it would be possible for a very little to get on it. I should not expect much.' That, he added, was still his opinion.

Cross-examined by Abinger, he admitted that he had not seen the body, nor the place where it had lain. Abinger then reminded him of Dr Needham, the other pathologist, who had visited the Common and described a scene of butchery. All that blood, said Abinger, a blood-stained jemmy dripping with blood, eight blows, one after the other – surely such violence could not have been done without leaving the evidence of yet more blood on the overcoat of the man who had struck those blows?

'I should not modify the opinion I have given, because those blows would be rapidly rained, and the tissues would be crushed at the time. There would not be much bleeding at the time the blows were delivered. The blood would ooze out afterwards.'

'The crowbar must have been dripping with blood?'

'There would be some blood on it,' said Wilcox reluctantly.

It can hardly be disputed that Abinger got more profit out of the last two witnesses than did Muir and Leycester. A few pin-points of blood on the collar of a soiled shirt were ludicrously insufficient to prove that Morrison, the owner of the shirt, was the man who had battered Leon Beron to death; much more strikingly do they suggest a lack of proof. And, despite the expert evidence of the senior scientific analyst of the Home Office, there must remain in the lay mind a stubborn belief that where blood is copiously shed the murderer will not leave the scene of the crime unstained.

NINE

The cab at Clapham Cross

OPENING his case for the defence, Abinger early showed his uneasy feeling that he had to defend himself as well as his client. He began, justifiably, by contrasting the enormous resources of the Crown with the scanty help available to the poor man whom he represented; but then spoke resentfully of some remark made by Muir on the previous day. He was sure, of course, that Mr Muir had not meant to be unkind, but he, Abinger, had felt the slur when he was accused of wasting the Court's time. The jury could be assured, he said, that he had not put a single question which he did not consider necessary, and now – so far from wasting time on analysis of the evidence for the prosecution – he was at once going to declare and explain his own case.

The jury would want to know where the accused had been on the night of 31 January, on the morning of the next day and on the days that followed. The prosecution had said he disappeared, but the fact was that he had remained quite openly in

Whitechapel. The story of the murder was in all the papers, there was a hue and cry for the murderer, but Morrison had 'stood his ground', and when arrested he was quietly having his breakfast in a restaurant only a stone's throw from the Warsaw.

That was a good point to make, for certainly Morrison had had the means and the opportunity – both money and time – to escape if he had wanted to escape, and thought flight necessary. Freedom of movement was still unhampered by the need to carry a passport, the recurrent need to apply for a visa, and he could have gone abroad and vanished as Peter the Painter had vanished. But he 'stood his ground', and still one must wonder why. Nothing but innocence – innocence whole and entire – could have justified his decision, and it is not easy to believe that Morrison had no knowledge of, or association with, what had been done and those who did it. Ignorance, however, is some-times the poor man's ragged substitute for innocence, and the conventions of guilt are neither uniform nor universal: the crimes of Clapham are notoriously chaste in Martaban. It is possible – and the possibility will have to be considered – that Morrison, by ignorance, was deluded into a sensation of innocence that Britannic law did not recognise.

Having made his point, Abinger then let emotion carry him into an extravagance of thought and diction. He was going to call the prisoner, he said, 'and he will have to go through an ordeal more terrible, I suggest, than the ordeal heretics had to undergo in the days of the Inquisition'. In cross-examination Muir could be formidable indeed, and even brutal, but Morrison was not the sort of man to whom a bullying counsel would seem more terrible than the ritual flames of a Spanish bonfire; and Abinger, on second thoughts, may have felt the comparison ill-suited to the occasion. He offered another, and suggested that a contest between a counsel so brilliant and a man of manifestly imperfect education would be as unequal 'as a fight between a professional prize-fighter and a curate'. It is doubtful, however, if that elicited for his client as much sympathy as he had hoped; for among the jurymen there must have been some who – looking at Steinie and remembering the curates they had known – found the similitude unconvincing.

The prisoner would tell them, said Abinger, that on the thirty-first he had been selling cheap jewellery in the city, and about eight o'clock he went to Snelwar's restaurant to have his supper. From there he walked to the Shoreditch Empire of Varieties, where he was seen by witnesses who would be produced, and from the Empire returned to the restaurant to pick up the flute he had left with the waiter called Mintz. Then Abinger provoked a long, unhappy and very tedious argument with Mr Justice Darling, for Mintz was the wretched man who had tried to commit suicide, and Abinger, in cross-examination of him, had already invited a warning from his lordship. Abinger, still smarting and still convinced that his cross-examination had been right and proper, began again to defend himself rather than the prisoner. 'My lord', he said, 'thought I was accusing the man Mintz of a felony, attempting to commit suicide – '

His lordship interrupted and carefully explained that what he had previously said was intended to remind Abinger that he might be exposing his client to an unsuspected danger: 'You pursued that cross-examination in such a way as to make it perfectly clear to my mind that you were imputing to that man something against his character. The fact that you did that (I mentioned the Criminal Evidence Act to you at the time) entitled Mr Muir to cross-examine the defendant, if he went into the witness-box, as to his character. That is what I meant, and I did not know if you appreciated it.'

'My lord,' said Abinger, 'I was familiar with the Act of Parliament, if I may say so. It is a very short time since it was passed. Gentlemen, my lord even now, if I may most respectfully say so, does not appreciate the real object of those questions – '

'It was not a question of what was your object,' said his lordship. 'The question I had in my mind was what Mr Muir would claim to do because of your questions, no matter with what object you put them. It was perfectly obvious to me that he would claim upon that to cross-examine the defendant as to his character.'

'I am aware of that,' said Abinger. 'That has been held as a rod over my head ever since this case started.' He became slightly incoherent as he tried to insist that, so far from trying to discredit

Mintz's character, he was merely establishing the unreliability, as a witness, of a man who had lately been in a lunatic asylum. That was a delicate and pretty distinction, but Abinger over-elaborated and obscured it. He said again, 'The rod has been held over me until it is insupportable. I was threatened by my lord – '

His lordship, not unreasonably, objected to the word 'threat-ened', but was patiently silent when Abinger, now openly dis-respectful, exclaimed 'Your lordship might have given me credit, after practising in these Courts for twenty-five years, for knowing a statute which every student of law must know.'

He turned to the jury and said, 'I knew what I was about, gentlemen, when I put those questions. I weighed the conse-quences.' Then, exposing the emotion he undoubtedly felt, and felt too deeply for his own good, asked, 'Can you picture to yourselves the anxiety that counsel has in a case of this sort? Was the jury to know that that man was a lunatic or not?' One sympathises with him, and admires his lordship's restraint. Abinger clearly thought himself entitled to discredit, on the grounds of character, witnesses for the prosecution without exposing Morrison to the peril of similar cross-examination; and Mr Justice Darling, having done what he could to disabuse him of that dangerous belief, retired into patient silence.

Abinger continued his statement, and said that after picking up his flute – or the parcel said to contain a flute – Morrison returned to his lodging. On his way there he saw Beron talking to a tall man at the corner of Sidney Street, and in his room at 91 Newark Street, where he lodged with people called Zimmerman, went to bed and remained there till morning, as the Zimmermans would testify. On the following morning he went to 116 York Road, and for some days lived there with Florrie Dellow, having deposited his revolver and ammunition at a railway cloakroom lest his possession of such things should frighten Mrs Dellow. He would prove, said Abinger, that Morrison had lately cashed a cheque for £35, thereby refuting the prosecution's story that the money he had on him, when he talked with the Flittermans in their kitchen, was the money of which he had robbed Beron. The blood-stained collar, which had aroused suspicion, had not been bought until 4 January, and as the prisoner, when arrested, had £14 in his pocket it was obvious that if he had wanted to leave the country he had sufficient means to let him do so. He would refrain, said Abinger, from pointing out that some of the prosecution's witnesses had 'practically admitted committing perjury', and that it would not be safe to rely on their evidence.

John Holmes Greaves, his first witness for the defence, was 'a medallist of the Royal Institution of British Architects', and a very solid man who gave convincing testimony – everything had been measured, everything was fully explained – about the house in Newark Street where Morrison had been living with the Zimmermans for three shillings a week and a penny a day for a glass of hot milk in the morning. The front door was fastened with two bolts, a night latch and a stop lock, and though only the upper bolt was in use – because the door was slightly sprung – it served, not merely to close the door, but as an alarm: it made a shrieking, grating noise when drawn, and would waken everyone in the house. There was a window in Morrison's ground-floor room, but it could only be opened with difficulty 'and a considerable amount of noise'.

Mr Greaves had also visited the cab-rank at Clapham Cross, at half-past one in the morning, where he discovered the virtual impossibility of clearly seeing, from the cab-rank, the features of anyone approaching from the direction of Old Street and the clock tower. Stephens the cabman had previously declared, 'I first saw my fare walking round the palings from the Old Town, Clapham. As he walked by me I asked him "Cab, sir?" He walked a little way on, and turned and came back to the cab, and told me to drive to Kennington.' Abinger, cross-examining, had asked, 'So that the light of the clock when he came towards your cab would be behind him?' To which the reply was 'Yes'; but Stephens added, 'He walked past the cab and said "Kennington", and then he got into the cab and I drove him there.'

Now in the witness box Mr Greaves gave his considered testimony: 'I came to the conclusion that for anyone to positively identify an individual, even if it were someone you knew, you had to place him in a certain position to get the light on him full in the face, and the only way to do that was to stand opposite to him with your back to the clock tower yourself, and with the individual under observation with his face to the clock tower so that you got the full light on his face.'

That was clear enough, though slightly repetitious, and under cross-examination Mr Greaves admitted that if a man, walking from the clock tower towards the cab-rank, had gone past Stephens' cab – then turned and come back to it – he would, for a moment at least, 'have had the light right in his face'. There is, then, a possibility that Stephens had caught a glimpse of the lighted face of the fare he picked up; and though he cannot be called a satisfactory witness he must be given the benefit of doubt, and that possibility granted.

The Zimmermans gave evidence that appeared to provide Morrison with an alibi sufficient to establish his innocence. He had, they said, gone to bed in their front room not long after midnight on the last day of the Old Year, and remained there till nine or ten in the morning, when he went out to wash in the yard. Maurice Zimmerman was a ladies' tailor, and Annie his wife was the mother of three children. They paid 6s 6d a week for two upstairs rooms at 91 Newark Street, and the kitchen and bedroom downstairs: Morrison had slept on a sofa in the down-stairs front room, and they had never gone to bed until he came in, after which the top bolt on the warped door was thrust home, and such was the noise it made that – on the night of the thirty-first or any other night – he could not have gone out again without wakening them. Of all the Whitechapel witnesses the Zimmer-mans seemed the most impressive – the most apparently reliable – and no attempt was made to impugn their respectability.

They had, they said – and so, with some bitterness, said Abinger – been interrogated again and again by the police, and seemingly their story had never varied. According to them Morrison was a man of regular habits, clean and tidy – Mrs Zimmerman used to take his linen to the laundry – and he was fond of the children and used to play with them. If the Zimmer-mans could be trusted, his alibi was almost perfect: the screaming door-bolt prevented him from going out, unheard, by the front door, though admittedly he might have opened the difficult, ill-hung window of his room without making any comparable noise.

There had been nothing in his behaviour, obvious to the Zimmermans, that suggested irregularity in his life except, perhaps, the fact that he had left behind three or four empty bottles of cherry brandy. He had, it is true, told them he was going to Paris when he left, but that, it seems, was his regular practice: when leaving one lodging for another, he always told his landlord or landlady that he had to go to Paris – though he was removing only to a nearby street – to avoid hurting their feelings.

Esther and Jane Brodsky, also called for the defence, were less convincing than the Zimmermans, and the case for the defence would have been stronger if Morrison's plea of alibi had been restricted to the hours after midnight on the thirty-first. But Morrison and his counsel were determined to show that he had not spent the evening of the thirty-first in company with Leon Beron, and to establish that attempted to prove, with unhappy result, that he had gone to the Shoreditch Empire of Varieties. There, said Esther Brodsky, she had seen him seated only a little distance away – he was in the same row, indeed – from where she and her sister had watched the performers and listened to their songs.

Both the Zimmermans had given their evidence with the help of an interpreter, supplied by the Court, but Esther, with an appeal for leniency that may or may not have been disingenuous, introduced herself by saying, 'I cannot speak much English. If you can understand me, I will speak, but I cannot understand much you say.' It was, perhaps, a convenient way of discounting the oath she had taken. She was twenty-three years old, she said, and lived with her sisters and her father – yet another tailor – at 71 Cleveland Street. She and her younger sister Jane went to the Shoreditch Empire on New Year's Eve, arriving about nine o'clock, and found seats in the orchestra stalls at the price of a shilling apiece. She could remember no particular singer or comedian who had contributed to the evening's entertainment, but she recognised the accused as the man who had sat not far from her. She had previously seen him passing their door in Cleveland Street, which was not far from Sidney Street and about ten minutes' walk from Newark Street.

It was a quarter or half past eleven when she and her sister left the Empire, Morrison having preceded them – they saw him 'at the door' – and going again on Monday, 2 January, they 'happened to sit next to him' and fell into conversation with him. Of that performance Esther remembered only that there had been a man who played the piano and sang a song; more memorable was the fact that Morrison walked home with them, and Esther reminded her sister that her birthday fell on the following Saturday. Morrison, with immediate gallantry, said he would like to call on them and bring 'a nice birthday present' for Jane. On that Monday night they could not ask him to come in – it was too late – and Jane said primly that she would not accept a present without her father's consent.

On Friday, between five and half past, Morrison called at the house in Cleveland Street, and with Mr Brodsky's permission gave Jane a little silver watch; then he took her and the youngest of the three sisters, Becky, to a pantomime at Forrester's Music Hall, returning at the respectable hour of nine. Cross-examined by Muir, Esther said that Jane had spoken to Morrison on three occasions only – on Monday the second, on Friday and Saturday of the same week – and so far as she knew there had been no talk of marriage between them. She had not discussed the matter with her sister, and though she remembered that Morrison had told her father he was a baker before taking to his present trade in cheap jewellery she had forgotten what else they talked about.

She was questioned again about the events of Saturday, New Year's Eve, and to both Muir and Mr Justice Darling repeated her assertion that she and Jane had gone to the Shoreditch Empire and seen Morrison there; and on the following Monday had found, by accident, seats beside him. Monday's performance was different from that they had seen on Saturday, but what they had, on either evening, she could not remember. She denied having gone to Brixton to visit Morrison in prison, and repeatedly declared that she did not know if Jane had been there. That assertion, despite reiteration, was received with some incredulity, and though Esther stoutly declared, 'I know what I say, and say what I know', it cannot be supposed that the jury were entirely convinced of her truthfulness.

Jane the younger sister, aged sixteen, was a much better

witness. She amplified the story that Esther had told, and said she had known Morrison, by sight, since before Christmas. He had been in the habit of passing their house in Cleveland Street, and on the afternoon of Saturday the thirty-first, when Jane slipped on the pavement, Morrison was there to catch her and save her from a fall. Jane, it is evident, was a quick-witted girl, and equally obvious is the fact that she had taken a fancy to the tall and handsome man who wore a look of distinction and a long, heavy overcoat. She claimed, moreover, to remember at least part of the performance she pretended to have seen on New Year's Eve: one of the comedians, she said, was Harry Champion, who wore a ginger wig and sang 'Ginger, you're balmy'. On Monday the second there was a different performance, about which she could speak with more authority: no Harry Champion, but Harry Harris, who played the piano and sang, and there was someone dressed as a Scotchman whose name she could not recall. She substantiated Esther's story of Morrison's visit to their house, to bring her a birthday present, and said the pantomime to which he took her and little Becky was *Babes in the Wood*. Then, on the following day, he called again, about four in the afternoon, and after some three hours with the family took her out to spend the evening in the house of people called Rotto in Fitzroy Square. From Cleveland Street they walked down the Mile End Road, took a motor-bus to the top of Tottenham Court Road and walked again to Fitzroy Square: the Rottos were 'grocery-shop people' whom she had not previously known.

About what happened in Fitzroy Square – the Rottos' house appears to have had a darker reputation than a grocery usually acquires – Jane was reticent and coy. When Muir asked if Morrison had made love to her, she answered, 'No, not exactly.'

'Not at all?' asked Muir.

'Never spoken,' said Jane unhappily. 'He has not spoken himself of love.'

'Has he spoken of marriage?' asked Muir with evident cynicism.

'He did not exactly say that. He asked me if I would give him permission to go with me and then marry me. I told him he had better ask father. Father said he would give him permission to go with me, but not to talk any rot into my head, as I was young yet.'

Like Eva Flitterman before her, Jane thought highly of marriage – and wished, very properly, to appear respectable – and it may, of course, have been Morrison's habit, or technique, to offer marriage as a preliminary to seduction. The improbability, as now it seems, of his having made a proposal on Friday the sixth, when he spoke to her for the second time, may not have been so improbable in the circumstances of London's East End in 1911; and, whatever the truth or untruth of her testimony, it is hardly to be doubted that Jane was urgently in love with Steinie, and it cannot be denied that she defended him with stubborn courage. The police had used her hardly. They may not have been unfair, and she made no complaint of brutality; but she had been subjected to long enquiry and severe pressure. Four or five times she had been taken to the Leman Street police station, and she had been questioned, sometimes at great length, about sixteen times. But she had neither weakened nor given in, and Muir himself could not make her recant though he brought evidence which apparently made nonsense of the only important part of her testimony: that she and her sister had seen Morrison at the Shoreditch Empire on New Year's Eve.

To begin with, she said, she had told the police nothing about their encounter, or near encounter, at the Empire, because they had not asked her, and she had not realised the value of such evidence. 'I told the police officers', she explained, 'that I did not know how to make a statement of my own accord, and if they would ask me questions I would answer them.' Later on, by her own admission, she was deliberately unco-operative because she felt she was being bullied, and she objected strongly to the frequent arrival of police officers at her door. The neighbours were talking about her, and on one occasion, when a constable arrived to take her to Leman Street, she made him walk on the farther pavement while she walked on the other. Then, when Inspectors Ward and Wensley asked if she had ever seen Morrison before their admitted meeting on the evening of Monday the second, she said she had, but it was no concern of theirs; and to Muir she excused or explained her behaviour with the ingenuous admission that she was angry with the police. She admitted, however, having told her story to Morrison's solicitor; and after his arrest she had been to see Morrison in prison.

Morrison, she said, had written and asked her to come and see him, but she was oddly reluctant to admit possession of his letter or letters. She did not know if she had kept them, but she would see. She was ready to swear to such improbable forgetfulness, but she would not swear that they were 'not at home somewhere'. Despite her fortitude and self-confidence, Jane, like other witnesses from the mean streets of Whitechapel, was constantly on guard, for ever aware that to tell the truth might be dangerous. Policemen in their sombre uniform and King's Counsel in their monstrous wigs were men who set traps for the unwary, and poor East Enders were their quarry. Jane, it may be, had more reason than most of the East Enders to be wary when questioned about her friendship with Steinie Morrison, for one cannot escape the thought that it was he who first conceived the notion of establishing an alibi for the early evening of 31 January, and persuaded Jane – who then persuaded her sister – to swear that they had seen him in the orchestra stalls of the Shoreditch Empire. Jane, in love with him, was an eager accomplice, and Esther, her dull sister, did what Jane told her to do. That, of course, is arrant guesswork, but too plausible to be lightly dismissed.

Wensley, it appears, had tried to make Jane admit to having known Morrison for five years; but refrained from pressing that suggestion when she told him that five years ago her age had been eleven. Then Mr Justice Darling intervened with a question about her evening with Morrison at the Rottos' house in Fitzroy Square, and with others about Florrie Dellow. He wanted to know how long she and Morrison had been together in the house, and if she had been alone with him.

'From half-past seven till ten o'clock?' he asked.

'About that time,' said Jane.

'Whereabouts were you during all that time?'

'In Rotto's house,' said Jane, stone-walling.

'Were you alone with him?'

'With him and Mrs Rotto.'

His lordship changed the subject and enquired if she had known anything of Florrie Dellow at that time.

'No.'

'Do you know now?'

'Reading the papers, I know who she is.'

'Did you know where he was living?'

'No.'

'Did he tell you where he lived?'

'No.'

'Did you ask?'

'I did not ask.'

'Was he proposing to marry you at that time?'

'Yes.'

'Had you agreed to marry him?'

'I told him I would see.'

'Did he spend money while he was out with you?'

'Not much.'

'On what sort of things did he spend money?'

'He paid for me to go to the Forrester's, and he paid my fare on the motor-bus.'

'Did he pay for refreshments anywhere?'

'No.'

'At Rotto's: did he pay for anything there, or were they friends of his?'

'Friends of his.'

From that dialogue Jane emerged with credit – she had said no more than she wanted to, she had accepted Steinie's association with Florrie Dellow and refused to show herself upset by it – and her examination was temporarily halted while Mr Roland Oliver, for the defence, called Max Mannis, who traded as 'The Japanese Laundry'. He gave evidence of Mrs Zimmerman's traffic with him, who used to bring her lodger Morrison's washing for his attention. He remembered various items she had brought, and displayed a lofty temper when questioned about police enquiries: 'The first time the police officers came they asked me whether I noticed blood on the things when they came to the wash, and I said, "I do not take notice of that, I could not examine all the things that come into the place." When parcels of linen come I open them, but I only examine the number – I do not take notice of any stains. If there were blood on the linen that came to me I would see it, but I do not take notice of that.' The Japanese Laundry, one infers, operated with oriental detachment from the misadventures and vulgarity of its customers.

One would be glad to know more of Max Mannis, but his testimony came abruptly to an end when Muir, who had received information of dramatic importance, interrupted to ask permission to recall Esther Brodsky and keep her sister out of Court while she was being interrogated. Permission being granted, Esther was again questioned about her attendance at the Shoreditch Empire on New Year's Eve. She repeated her sworn statement that she and her sister had found seats, and paid a shilling apiece for them.

Then Muir exploded his discovery of her perjury. 'I want to put this to you,' he said, 'that that being New Year's Eve, the lowest price for the stalls was one shilling and sixpence. Are you not making a mistake?'

'No,' said Esther, 'I am not making any mistake. I am certain what I paid. I could not tell you what the prices were at the time, but I know what I paid. I cannot remember whether I took tickets or whether my sister paid.'

His lordship enquired: 'Either you or your sister paid the two shillings at the box office?'

'At the box office.'

'I put it to you that that was impossible,' said Muir.

'Then it must come out that I am a liar, if you speak the truth.'

'It does. Exactly!'

'Well, I speak the truth,' said Esther. 'I know we paid a shilling.'

Then Jane was recalled, who told – but more explicitly – the same story as her sister. They had gone to the theatre at nine o'clock, just as the curtain was going up, and were in time to get the last two vacant seats, for which they paid a shilling each.

'Do you know', asked Muir, 'that the price was raised for orchestra stalls to one and sixpence each?'

'I do not know that,' said Jane.

'And that you could not have got in at nine o'clock, or any other time, for a shilling?'

'I know I got in!'

'Before nine o'clock', said Muir, 'there were no seats left in the house, and people were standing.'

'People may have been standing,' said Jane, 'but I got two vacant seats.'

Re-examined by Abinger, she said she had not been in the habit of going to music-halls. Saturday, indeed, was the very first time she had been in one, and she had got her father's approval before going. She gave the impression that she was a girl who would do nothing of which her father disapproved.

From the newspapers, she admitted, she had learnt that Morrison was living with Florrie Dellow, and when Abinger asked if she had come voluntarily to speak on his behalf she retorted with spirit, 'I come here to tell the truth. I come to say nothing that I do not know, but all that I know.'

When she was first questioned by the police she knew that Morrison was suspected of murder, but she had not spoken of seeing him at the Empire, on the evening before murder was committed, because she had not thought it of importance, either to him or the police. The police, moreover, had asked when she first knew Morrison, and that was very confusing; 'For I cannot say that I know anybody if I have not spoken to anybody.'

Brushing that aside, Muir said to her, 'You had heard' – so she had told him – 'that the crime was committed at midnight, and you knew where Morrison was up to eleven o'clock?'

'Eleven o'clock', said Jane, 'is not midnight.'

'Before this time he had already asked you if you would marry him?'

'Yes.'

She denied having said anything designed to help him – 'I only said what I knew' – and then she was asked if she concealed from the police her pretended memory of having seen Morrison at the Empire because, in fact, 'You never saw him there at all?'

'I did see him,' she said. 'I swear that I saw Morrison there on the night of 31 December. Nobody can deny my own eyes.'

Not until she read in the papers that Snelwar had said Morrison spent the evening in his restaurant did she realise the importance of denying his statement; and then, on the advice of a friend in her workshop, she had gone to see Steinie's lawyer. And still, she said, she had told the police nothing for the good, feminine reason that she was angry with them.

Perjury, of course, is not merely a sin, but a great nuisance. How simple would a government find its task of administration if all its subjects were honest, and how easily would policemen find, and the law convict, the criminals who oppress society if witnesses could be depended on to tell the truth! Whether judged by ethical or pragmatic standards, perjury must be condemned out of hand – and still one cannot help admiring the resolute perjurer who, not for his or her own advantage, but to save another sinner from the gallows, refuses to yield to incontrovertible demonstration of his falsity, and persists in declaring that a manifest lie is simple truth! Illiterate though they were, the Brodsky girls, being Jewish, must have known the meaning of an oath, but turned their backs upon the truth to be true to an older convention of loyalty – Jane to Steinie Morrison, Esther to Jane – and nothing more clearly reveals the strength and charm of Steinie's own personality than this discovery of his ability to enlist such loyalty. The Brodsky girls could not disarm the heavy assault of proven fact, but from Muir's harsh proof of fact they did not retreat but stood – upright in their faith and totally at fault – in defence of the indefensible.

The next witness was more cautious and seemed, at first, reluctant to commit himself to positive statement. Ernest Melbourne Edward Lewis was a clerk in the Capital and Counties Bank and testified that on 2 December, in the Commercial Road branch where he was a cashier, a man came in and asked for banknotes in exchange for £35 in cash. He would not, however, identify the accused as that man – 'I do not know that it is the business of bank clerks to know people's faces' – though he admitted the close resemblance between Morrison's signature, as shown him in Court, and the handwriting on the exchange slip that his customer had given him: 'I should say', he said nervously, 'that the signatures were signed by the same man.'

Muir cross-examined briefly – Lewis confirmed what he had

previously said – and Muir, harking back to the disputed shape of the 'S'-like cuts on Leon Beron's dead cheeks, suggested that 'The "S" in the handwriting shown here today is made differently to what it is on the exchange slip?' And Lewis agreed.

'The "S" on the exchange slip is very open,' said Muir, 'like the open thing in a fiddle?'

Either Lewis knew what he meant by 'the open thing in a fiddle', or was in a hurry to get out of the witness-box and knew that unequivocal agreement promised the quickest exit; for again he said 'Yes', and to some of the jury it may have seemed that another step, short and hastily measured though it was, had been taken towards identifying Morrison with the murderer of Leon Beron.

Isabel Saunders, a spinster living with a married sister near Clapham Common, spoke of her discovery of a blood-stained handkerchief on the Common at half-past eight on the morning of 2 January. It lay near the railings at the end of the path leading from the bandstand, it caught her eye as she passed, and dutifully she took it to Scotland Yard. But Miss Saunders' testimony seems to have elicited little interest, and contributed nothing to solution of the essential puzzle.

Then Abinger called William Whiddett, a short-sighted taxi-driver, whose sight was corrected by spectacles, who commonly stood on the Clapham Common rank, and contradicted the evidence of the cab-drivers previously called by saying that drivers rarely looked at, or took much notice of their fares, and by reason of their lack of interest would be unlikely to recognise them at a later date. He was followed by another taxi-driver, Frederick Stalden Crocher, who agreed that he took no particular interest in his passengers, and after a lapse of ten days would be unlikely to recognise a fare, by his clothing or appearance, unless his attention had been directed towards him by unusual circumstances.

A salesman in a hosiery shop testified to the selling of some underclothing, collars and shirts to a customer on 4 January, whom he doubtfully recognised as the prisoner in the dock; and then Florrie Dellow was called. She was, she said, a married woman, separated from her husband, and lived in a bedsitting-room at 116 York Road, for which she paid 6s 6d a week. Her

landlord was Mr Frank, and on the floor above her lived Mr and
Mrs Hall; Florrie could evidently afford to pay for domestic
service, and Mrs Hall did her washing, cooking and other work.
She had first met Morrison about midday on 1 January when
Frank, who had previously spoken of him, introduced him to
her.

'You look lonely,' said Morrison – an admirable approach –
and promptly asked her if she would like to live with him.
Florrie, if she spoke the truth, wasted no more time than Steinie,
but answered 'Yes, if you will look after me'. He said he would
and, having politely asked Frank's permission to move in, spent
that Sunday night with her. He left the next morning, between
ten and eleven o'clock, but returned on Tuesday, and in the
growth of familiarity told her that he made his living by selling
cheap jewellery. That night she could not let him stay, for she
had made arrangements to accommodate a friend of established
status, but on Wednesday he came again, about midday, bringing
his luggage in a cab, and from then till the following Saturday
slept in her room. Then Florrie was again compelled to dis-
appoint him – again, by previous arrangement, an old friend was
coming to see her – and Morrison most obligingly said it didn't
matter and, before leaving her, put on clean clothes. He had been
to the nearby public baths, and Mrs Hall, from the floor above,
had joined them while he was changing his linen. Florrie put
cuff-links in his shirt, and threw some dirty clothes into a basket
under her bed. Steinie, it seemed, suffered from occasional
bleeding of the nose, and on Thursday morning, said Florrie –
she thought it was Thursday – she had seen blood flowing. But
on Sunday morning, in Steinie's absence, she realised that their
brief friendship had come to an end when her room was invaded
by three detectives, one of them Inspector Ward, who locked her
door and settled down to make search for all they could find
that belonged, or may have belonged, to her casual lover.

Now Florrie was faced by Muir in his most pugnacious mood.
'You have lived six months in this house?' he asked.

'Yes,' she said.

'Do you take men home there?'

'I have a few friends which visit me.'

'With the knowledge of Mr Frank?'

'Well, he knows.'

'And Mrs Hall?'

'Mrs Hall knows certainly. Yes.'

'That you take different men home there?'

'My friends. I do not take different men. I have my friends there.'

'You are a common prostitute, are you not?'

'I beg pardon, no.'

'You have been convicted?'

'I might have been. That is nothing to do with this case, is it?'

'For prostitution in the street?'

'Yes,' said Florrie, as indifferent as Muir himself to the latent impropriety of his question.

Destruction of her character was followed by very tedious enquiry about the contents of Morrison's collar-box – the search for blood-stains was unrewarded – and a very curious inquisition into Florrie's knowledge of where Morrison had previously lived, from which it emerged that she did not know her way to Tottenham Court Road. She came originally from somewhere in Lincolnshire, but for the last three years, before removing to York Road, had been living in Westminster Bridge Road.

'Do you think', asked Muir, 'that Tottenham Court Road is in the East End?'

'I can't tell you,' she answered, and hazarded, 'It's in the City, isn't it?' London was still an agglomeration of villages, and the villagers knew very little about their neighbours.

While Morrison lived with her, Florrie – if she spoke the truth – had not been much enriched by their association. By about £2, she said. She had, however, seen banknotes that he carried, and it is not improbable that she minimised her earnings, as prudence must have dictated.

After Morrison's arrest she had visited him in prison: every day except Saturday, she said, she had gone to see him, and so had Mrs Hall and an old lady called Mrs Wheeler who lived in an upper room at the house in York Road. Frank, too, their disreputable landlord had gone, though not in company with them. That Morrison had the gift of attracting and acquiring friends cannot be doubted, though the character of his friends may not elicit much admiration.

To Abinger Florrie told – without apparent advantage to his case – the sad little tale of her life: her husband had deserted her, she had no means of support except her father's occasional bounty – he was a publican – and while her mother looked after two of her children she supported a third on the wages of prostitution. At one time, she said, she had been on the stage, but not for very long, and had abandoned the theatre for the unrewarding state of matrimony. Except for charges of soliciting, she had been in no trouble with the police.

Her neighbour, Mrs Anna Hall, admitted to having done some cooking and washing for Florrie, and on the first Saturday of the New Year, going into Florrie's room, she had watched Morrison changing his clothes. The police had not questioned her, but twice she had gone to Brixton Prison to visit Morrison 'because I thought I would like to see him'.

Cross-examined by Muir, she said she had been in their room several times while Morrison was dressing, and his habit was to change his underclothes once a week. She was not aware that Florrie took men home to sleep with her, but thought she had 'two or three gentlemen callers'. Whether they spent the night with Florrie she could not say – 'I never troubled about that, my place being in my own husband's home' – and never had she gone to visit them in the early morning.

'How is it you favoured the accused by going in when he was dressing?' asked Muir.

'Well, I believed they were going to knock their heads together,' said Mrs Hall. 'That they were going to live together as man and wife.'

As other witnesses had done, she stoutly asserted her respectability, and there is no reason to doubt the probity of the two warders from the prison at Brixton by whom she was followed. Their purpose was to testify to having seen Morrison's nose bleeding, and his request that they should take note of his embarrassing disability. There was, after all, an innocent explanation – should one be needed – of those pin-points of blood on his collar.

TEN

Steinie Morrison in the dock at the Old Bailey

THE Criminal Evidence Act of 1894 permitted a prisoner to give evidence on his own behalf; and when, in the afternoon of the fifth day of the trial, Steinie Morrison was called into the box it was to enact a new role as leading witness for the defence.

It can hardly be doubted that Abinger was aware of the danger he invited. His cross-examination of the waiter Mintz – who had, at least once, tried to commit suicide – may be defended on the grounds that he was not attacking Mintz's character, but attempting to show that he was mentally unbalanced and his evidence was therefore untrustworthy. The questions put to Mrs Deitch, however, were manifestly intended to undermine her testimony by exposing her as a woman of immoral character; and by attacking her in that way he left Morrison open to like attack. About that the Criminal Evidence Act was perfectly clear, and – it might be argued – equally unfair. The case for the prosecution did not

126

entirely depend on Mrs Deitch's evidence, and to discredit her would not demolish it; but Morrison's character, as a witness, was of far greater importance, and it is possible that Abinger still thought – or hoped – that he could protect his client against Muir's cross-examination by interposing, like a shield, a romantic demand for fair play. Morrison, it seems, had insisted on Abinger's cross-examination of both Mintz and Mrs Deitch; and Abinger was apparently persuaded to accept an obvious risk because he believed Morrison to be an innocent man whose innocence the Court would recognise.

Morrison, on oath, said he had been born in Australia and was between twenty-nine and thirty years of age. He spoke of his employment by Mr Pithers, the baker of Lavender Hill, and of leaving Pithers when he received a letter to say his father was ill, and he decided to go home; whether to Australia or to Russia remained obscure. Then came another letter – his father's health had improved – and instead of going to Moscow or Melbourne he bought a stock of cheap jewellery and travelled with that. After leaving Lavender Hill he spent two days at 4 Whitfield Street, from there went to 5 Grove Street, where his rent was three shillings a week, and on the last Friday in November to the Zimmermans at 91 Newark Street. He was earning about £2 a week, seldom less, and towards the end of November he became much richer when his mother, in Russia, sent him £20.

He spent it with some extravagance: £2 for a suit of clothes; an eighteen-carat gold watch and chain decorated with a half-sovereign (receipt dated 30 November) for £9 17s 6d; on the same day an overcoat for £2; on 2 December a mackintosh, £1 17s 6d; and some smaller items from Hope Brothers for £3 5s 5½d. At a sale in Aldgate a revolver and a box of ammunition cost him seven or eight shillings, and in vain he had tried to sell them at the Warsaw for twelve shillings. On 2 December, moreover, he exchanged thirty-five sovereigns for banknotes at the Capital and Counties Bank in Commercial Road. At a club in Greenfield Street, he explained, he had had a lucky run at faro, winning £28 on an initial capital of £10, and after handsomely giving the croupier £3 he had left the club with £35 in his pocket. On 23 December he pawned the watch he had bought, though he was in no need of money, and during those weeks while he was living in Grove Street and Newark Street he acquired the habit of eating at Snelwar's Warsaw Restaurant, sometimes going there three times a day, but sometimes missing a day or two.

At the Warsaw he met Leon Beron, whom he and everyone else knew as 'the landlord'.

'Did you kill that man?' asked Abinger.

'No, I did not.'

Beron, said Morrison, 'was always there, as well as his brother'; but he had never seen him in possession of any large sum of money. As for his watch, anyone could see that, for 'whenever he was sitting down by the table, his coat was always open'. Otherwise Beron would walk up and down, talking to the customers. Morrison had never handled his watch, never gone to see him at his rooms in Jubilee Street, nor had Beron visited him.

Carefully and laboriously Abinger elicited from his witness the details of his daily habit, the small events of his life: how he tried to sell jewellery and his pistol at the Warsaw, and saw Jack Taw there, 'loafing about all day long', and one day, passing Frank's shop, noticed him 'in the window, repairing watches', and pausing for conversation learnt that Florrie Dellow was also for sale. On Sunday morning he used to wear his best suit of clothes, and Mr Justice Darling was irritated by Abinger's insistence on knowing how often he put on a clean collar, how many he owned. 'What's the point?' demanded his lordship.

'The point', said Abinger – lunging wildly and off-balance – 'is that a man who had got six or seven clean collars is not likely to be wearing the same blood-stained collar that he was wearing on the night of a bloody murder committed eight days before.'

With stubborn patience Abinger continued his examination. Morrison's hats and boots were of equal interest to him; he wanted to know, precisely, the shortest way from Snelwar's restaurant in Osborn Street to the Zimmermans' house in Newark Street. He enquired when Steinie got up in the morning, what use he made of his latchkey; and then, more dramatically, if he had ever owned a dagger, five or six inches long, or a weapon 'which has been described as a bar of iron'?

According to Joe Mintz, the suicidal waiter, it was on 31 December, a little after six o'clock, that Morrison gave him for safe-keeping 'a parcel about two feet long and wrapped up in brown paper'. Morrison had said it contained a flute, but Mintz thought it felt like a bar of iron. Now Morrison told Abinger that on the thirty-first he had bought a flute, for four shillings or four and sixpence, at a stall in Aldgate – 'on the left-hand side as you come out of Whitechapel into Aldgate' – between ten and eleven in the morning, which was not long after he had breakfasted at the Warsaw. And there, said Morrison, he had had a little dispute with Mintz, who, chattering in the kitchen, had kept him waiting for a quarter of an hour. 'I shouted out to him, "Hullo, what are you doing down there? Are you trying to hang yourself again?" Upon which he ran out of the kitchen and served me. But he told me, "If ever I get the chance to get it out of you, I will." And I believe he is doing it now.'

That, indeed, seems not improbable. Morrison had made a brutal joke, and Mintz, as sensitive as a scalded child, had seen his opportunity for revenge. Or someone, perhaps, had cleverly pointed to an opportunity and persuaded him to take it. It was easy enough to pretend that a flute, wrapped in brown paper, looked like a bar of iron, easy to say it felt as heavy. It would be less easy, of course, to suppose that a purposive murderer was likely to leave his intended weapon on the counter of a restaurant, such as the Warsaw, until he was ready to pick it up and take it away; but in the Warsaw stark improbability and perjury appear to have been equally at home. Habitués shrank from neither.

In Cleveland Street, early one afternoon, Morrison made the acquaintance of Jane Brodsky who was standing at the garden gate as he passed, and 'happened to slip' as she came out: 'She accidentally knocked into me, and I apologised.' A brief encounter, but it was to have consequences. Then Abinger spoke of another of Morrison's friends, dim-witted Eva Flitterman, whom he had met at Christmas time. Eva in the witness-box had talked of marriage and wanted to be thought respectable, but he had found her in 'a prostitutes' house' in Harding Street, and taking her home with him to Newark Street, where she complained of the cold, he gave her five shillings and a green scarf worth half-a-crown. That was a digression, however, and Abinger quickly returned to the Warsaw, the evening of the thirty-first and the matter of the brown paper parcel.

It was about eight o'clock when he went in, said Morrison, and Snelwar's little daughter – to whom he used to give fruit – had run to meet him and ask what was in the parcel. 'A flute,' he said, and giving it to Mintz, who stood behind the counter, asked him to keep it for him till he returned from the Shoreditch Empire. He had a meal – 'a substantial tea', if he remembered rightly – and among the thirty or forty people in the restaurant noticed Solomon Beron. He was not sure if Leon had been there too, and most certainly he and Leon had not been sitting together at nine o'clock, nor had they gone out together at a quarter to twelve. Emphatically, too, he denied the evidence of Hermilin the furrier who said he had seen Morrison take Leon Beron's watch – that conspicuous timepiece – and heard him, as he held it in his hands, comment on its impressive weight. Never, said Morrison, had he done any such thing: neither handled the watch nor – if memory served him – spoken of its heaviness.

It was half past eight when he left the restaurant, to go to the Empire, where he arrived before the nine o'clock performance began, and put down half a sovereign to pay for his seat. A shilling was the usual price, but he could not remember how much change he got, and he may have paid one and sixpence. He was fond of the Shoreditch Empire, and always went to the same place in the stalls. He remembered, moreover, some of the turns: 'There was an actress, I believe it was Gertie Gitana. There was Harry Lauder.'

For some unknown reason that assertion stirred Mr Justice Darling's attentive mind to scepticism, and when questioned by him Morrison admitted that his memory was not so positive as he had pretended: he could not exactly remember, though 'there was a gentleman dressed up as a Scotchman, and he spoke in the language of a Scotchman too'. And sitting not far from him, in the stalls, was Jane Brodsky, whom he noticed 'because of her good looks'; but he spoke neither to her nor her sister, and leaving the Empire, at some time after eleven o'clock, returned to Snelwar's restaurant at about a quarter to twelve.

There, with initially an accent of doubt in his voice, he thought he remembered seeing Leon Beron: 'It is quite possible that I believe I did. I do not think he was sitting down: he nearly always stands up most of the time.'

His lordship, with authority in his voice, called him to attention and asked, 'Do you remember seeing him there on that night?' And Morrison, responding to authority, answered, 'Yes.'

He described the amenities of the restaurant: 'As you go in there is a bar where cakes, bread and butter and so forth are exhibited. Farther into the restaurant are about fourteen or fifteen tables.' And anyone can go in and sit down where he likes.

But he did not sit down at the same table with Beron – 'No, of course I did not' – he had a cup of tea and a piece of cake, and then he went to the bar and asked for his flute; he put it in his pocket, and drank a glass of lemonade. He was wearing a brown motor-cap – exhibited in Court – and brown boots with very light spats. It would be about 11.45 or 11.50 when he left the restaurant.

The Court adjourned, and when, in the late afternoon of the following day – the sixth day of the trial – it adjourned again, Steinie Morrison was still under cross-examination.

II

That long, sixth day began with his assertion that, on leaving the restaurant, he walked along Whitechapel Road till he came to Cambridge Road, and there crossed over to Sidney Street. At the corner of Sidney Street someone shouted, 'Bonsoir, M'sieur', and looking round he saw Leon Beron standing with a very tall, well-dressed man on the other side of the street; but he could not see the face of the tall man. He continued on his way to Newark Street, saw a woman at the door of number 93, and at the next house – the Zimmermans' – let himself in with his latch-key and went to bed. There he remained until after nine o'clock on Sunday morning, when he got up and went to the public baths in Sidney Square. He had breakfast at the restaurant in Fieldgate Street – where a week later he was arrested – and after a brief visit to the Warsaw walked to Westminster Bridge, crossed it and at 116 York Road was introduced to Florrie Dellow by

Frank the pimping watchmaker. Having established friendly relations with her, he returned to Newark Street, packed his clothes and – to avoid giving offence – told Mrs Zimmerman that he had to go to Paris. He deposited his revolver at the cloak-room at St Mary's railway station – lest it frighten Florrie Dellow – and to pass the time paid a visit to the Flittermans. There he joined a family party, for as well as Eva her sisters and mother were there, her brothers and some brothers-in-law; and for Isaac Flitterman Morrison cashed a cheque, giving him in exchange eight half-sovereigns. Then he returned to York Road, and spent the night with Mrs Dellow.

With minute particularity Abinger insisted on plotting Morrison's movements to and fro in that warren of mean streets, and drew from him every detail of his small, inconsequential activities: how, on Sunday morning, he had put on clean linen and his green suit, 'the one I am wearing now'; how he had waited till Mrs Zimmerman heated a glass of milk for him; how, after breakfasting in Fieldgate Street, he had looked into the Warsaw to ask if anyone had seen a regular customer known as 'the Colonial', but had not tarried there; how, a day or two after Christmas, he had called on Frank to discuss his promised introduction to Florrie Dellow – and by so doing bored and perplexed the jury, whose Foreman at last interrupted to ask his lordship, 'My lord, are we to try all this? These details seem to me quite unnecessary.'

More than once, during the trial, the Foreman tried to play a more active part in the proceedings than his position warranted, but on this occasion his lordship, also bored by the endless elaboration of Abinger's questions, showed his sympathy and said that he saw no necessity for such minute exposure of detail.

Abinger, however, knew what he was doing, and could show reason for it. It had been suggested, he said, that Morrison, after committing murder, had disappeared. But, so far from that being true, he had remained in Whitechapel and 'stood his ground'. His behaviour, his inaction, had been strange indeed: to neglect, as he had done, wide-open opportunities for escape could hardly be explained except by presumption of his innocence; but Abinger spoiled a valid argument by pursuing it with too much excitement.

He intended, he said, to show forth Morrison's life throughout the week in which London was 'ransacked' to discover Beron's murderer. Morrison, reading the papers, knew what was going on, but still 'stood his ground'. To the best of his humble judgment, said Abinger, that was an important fact, 'not from the point of view of the prosecution, but from the point of view of the accused'.

'Are you addressing the jury,' asked his lordship, 'or what are you doing?'

'I am addressing your lordship.'

'There is no need to address me on a point like this in such a rhetorical strain.'

'If your lordship rules –'

'I rule nothing of the kind,' said his lordship testily. He and the jury were prepared to listen to a plain tale of what Morrison had been doing, but there was no need to describe every minor occurrence; for 'there is this to be borne in mind, that he will be cross-examined, and if there is anything more that is desired to be known he will be asked about it then'. So, at a quickened pace, the tale was resumed, from the Shoreditch Empire and the Miss Brodskys to Florrie Dellow, and from his purchase of six collars to arrest in Fieldgate Street. During his interrogation Morrison said that, although he knew there had been a murder on Clapham Common, he did not realise that the murdered man was someone he had known. The name Leon Beron meant nothing to him, for at Snelwar's restaurant Beron was called 'the landlord', and he, Morrison, had never heard his real name. He described in detail his arrest, and again the Court heard that he had been accused of murder.

Abinger asked how many policemen came into the restaurant where he was taking his breakfast, and Morrison replied: 'Three of them jumped in at once, but there were one or two afterwards. I was seized at once by two, and the third one, Inspector Wensley, caught hold of my arm. Inspector Wensley said to me, "Steinie, I want you for murder." The other two officers at once started rubbing their hands along my sides. I did not know what it was for. I thought they were going to put something in my pockets, and I said to them, "Please don't put anything in my pockets."

My pockets were searched in the restaurant, and then I was taken through the streets. One detective held my left arm and another detective held my right arm; Inspector Wensley was within a foot or two behind me, and the other two were following up.'

At the police station, he declared, Wensley said to him, ' "You will be detained at present, but you will be charged with murder when Inspector Ward comes." I was then put in an open cell. All my clothes were taken away from me – everything bar the pants, socks and vest – and they gave me some blankets to put on.' He slept in the Leman Street police station, and on the following day, when witnesses – most of them from the Warsaw – were called in to identify him, he had to stand 'among nine or ten persons, every one of whom was very shabbily dressed'.

Abinger concluded his examination, and Muir began cross-examination by asking Morrison how much money he had on him when he joined the Flittermans' family party on New Year's Day, and that led to a long series of questions about the source or sources of Steinie's income. It was his habit, it appeared, to carry both gold and banknotes: banknotes were more convenient, but he needed gold because, in his way of life, he met people who would ask him to cash a cheque for them, and pay sixpence or a shilling for the service.

He became indignant, however, when Muir asked if he could name any single person for whom he had cashed a cheque between 2 and 25 December. 'No, certainly not,' he answered. 'I never ask them their names.'

'Do you get their cheques?' asked Muir.

'Certainly.'

'With their names on them?'

'Is it my business to look at their names? Their names are not on the cheque.'

Again Muir asked, 'Will you name any single person for whom you changed a cheque?' And, as if instructing a poor foreigner, from some remote part of the world, in the basic facts of life in England, Morrison replied, 'But you will excuse me! The name of the person for whom I changed the cheque is not on the cheque.'

'You cashed those cheques at the bank?'

'Yes.'

'Can you bring any witness to prove that you cashed any cheque between 2 and 25 December?'

'If I had known that I would be arrested and accused of a crime that I had never committed I would certainly take the precaution to take the names of those people, but as I did not expect anything of the kind I naturally did not ask them for their name.'

'Will you name any bank where you changed the cheques that you got?'

'I did not even know the name of the bank in which I cashed the cheque – the very last one – for the simple reason that I did not look at it.'

One is left in considerable perplexity as to the nature of Morrison's financial transactions, and even Muir gave up his attempt to clarify them. He turned attention to the £38 that Morrison claimed to have won at faro, on or about 1 December, and asked if he could bring witnesses of his success.

The croupier, said Morrison. He could not say where the croupier lived, but he knew his name.

'Have you got any witnesses to corroborate your statement that you won money in a gambling-house on that date?'

'As I tell you, I can give you the name of the croupier.'

'Will you answer my question?' demanded Muir.

That was blatant bullying, and his lordship intervened to say 'He is trying to answer it'. But Muir was undeterred by rebuke, repeated his question and Morrison defiantly retorted that if a couple of policemen took him to the gaming-house he could call its occupants to give evidence on his behalf.

Sourly Muir enquired, 'Have you ever told this story of winning £38 in gold until you came to this Court?'

'No,' said Morrison. And cleverly added, 'For the simple reason that I did not wish the detectives to go and bully all my witnesses as they did to every one of them that have been present in Court up to now.'

No attempt was made, as it seems, to prove or disprove the existence of the gaming-house and a croupier who had paid out £38; and, without too much cynicism, one may suppose that the prosecution refrained from investigation for fear of finding them, while Abinger was averse from further enquiry for fear of not finding them.

Muir continued his cross-examination: 'You told us also that you got £20 from your mother?'

'Yes.'

'Where did the money come from?'

'From Russia.'

'What form did it come in?

'It came in two £5 notes and a £10 note, so far as I can remember.'

'English money?'

'English money, yes.'

'Have you got any letter that came with that money?'

'No.'

'Does that again depend entirely upon your word?'

'I destroyed that letter, for the simple reason that I did not wish to keep it with me.'

'Have you got any corroboration at all of your word that you got that £20 from Russia?'

Morrison could offer no corroboration other than the fact that he had, towards the end of November, spent about £20 on clothes and jewellery; and but for the fortuitous arrival of a handsome present he could not have afforded such lavish expenditure.

His explanation, apparently so ingenuous, did not exclude the possibility of his having received a substantial sum of money from another, unnamed source: a mother domiciled in Russia – presumably in humble circumstances – who was able to accumulate English banknotes to the value of £20, and post them to a son, now living in Whitechapel, whom she had borne somewhere in Australia, was not a character likely to inspire total and immediate belief. That such a tall, dashing, adventurous creature as Steinie – though lately living on the poor wages of a baker's labourer – could win £38 at faro was not incredible; but that Steinie had, in Muscovy, a mother who could at need display the power and tinsel of a fairy godmother strained credulity; and Muir was probably justified in pursuing, with angry intensity, his pitiless enquiry into the prisoner's expenditure at the end of November and in the early days of December. But, unexpectedly, his interrogation excited Abinger's opposition, who asked, 'To what issue is this examination directed?'

Said Muir: 'It is the possession of the money on 1 January which he attempts to account for in the way he has stated.'

'That is not the point I put,' said Abinger. 'I asked my friend what is the issue that this is directed to?'

'The issue', said Muir, 'is whether he was, on 1 January, in possession of the proceeds of the robbery of Leon Beron.'

'That', said Abinger, 'is cross-examination directed to the credit of the witness, and I object to it.'

Was his objection precipitated by emotion? At this distance in time it does appear that he had been waiting for the earliest opportunity to interrupt Muir's relentless and destructive cross-examination; for Muir, beyond question, had exposed the weakness of Steinie's claim to have acquired a considerable sum of money by innocent means. But perhaps he intervened too soon.

Muir may well have been wrong – I believe he was – wrong in supposing that Morrison's sudden affluence was the consequence of his robbing Beron of the money that Beron was believed to carry in his shabby pockets; but he was justified in throwing doubt on Morrison's unsubstantiated claim to have won £38 at faro, and his nonsensical pretence to have received £20, in English money, from a supposititious mother in Russia. But Muir was oddly at fault in ignoring the fact that Morrison may have received sums of money, amounting in all to nearly £60, from an unknown source for an undisclosed purpose; and Abinger, though he would refrain from such speculation, can hardly have closed his mind to the possibility of that having happened. It seems fairly certain that Morrison was remunerated at least once, and probably twice; but by whom was not discovered.

Abinger, that always well-meaning but sometimes ill-advised man, ran foul of Mr Justice Darling when he objected to Muir's cross-examination on the grounds that it was directed against the credit of his witness, and a very tedious long argument ensued. The Criminal Law Evidence Act of 1898 was again evoked, the testimony of Mintz and Mrs Deitch once more recalled – poor

Eva Flitterman and her perjury were pitilessly revived – and legal argument, of a sort that only lawyers could enjoy, was disinterred to bury evidence already entombed. Abinger, totally committed to defence of his client, was now unashamedly emotional; Mr Justice Darling was patient and judicious; and a seemingly interminable debate suddenly dissolved to let Muir repeat his enquiry: from whom or where had Morrison received the money of which he was in possession on 1 January?

Like a boxer who appears to have taken too much punishment and then, after a minute's rest, comes up freshly pugnacious, so Morrison seemed to have profited by the rest he had been given while his lordship expounded and explained the Criminal Evidence Act. Now, so far from defending himself against the charge of having money that he could not properly account for, he went over to the attack and claimed to have been richer by about £15 than anyone had previously suggested.

'Where did you get that from?' asked Muir.

He had saved about £4 while working as a baker, said Morrison, and the remainder – in addition to other money he had received before going to work at Lavender Hill – had been sent him from home.

'From your mother?' asked Muir.

'Yes,' said Morrison. As at a later date she had sent him English banknotes, but he had nothing to prove receipt of them. Of course he hadn't, though if he had thought it necessary to keep her letters he would certainly have done so. And, as to the gold albert he had pawned, he had come to the conclusion that he did not like it, and having pawned it for £4 10s he tried to sell the ticket for a sovereign in the hope – after chaffering had reduced his price – of earning five or ten shillings on it, 'as I very often do'.

There was, he admitted, nothing to show that between 23 December and 1 January he had spent any money at all, and his explanation of that deficiency was proud and simple: 'I have no document to show that I was spending money, for the simple reason that it was not necessary for me to buy anything whatever. I had everything I wanted, and it cost me twenty-five or thirty shillings a week to live on.' To further questioning he said he could explain his having some £24, on the day after Beron's murder – and prove his earlier possession of a substantial sum – by calling the Zimmermans to witness the fact that, while he was living with them, they had seen him, in their kitchen, displaying four or five – 'Or six, in fact' – £5 notes.

Defeated in his immediate purpose, Muir looked for a new topic, and found it in the person of the murdered man. Muir's intention, or hope, was to extract an admission from Morrison that he had been on friendly terms with Leon Beron, and to that end he could cite the testimony of Snelwar, proprietor of the Warsaw; Mintz the suicidal waiter; and Hermilin the furrier who lived above the restaurant. Morrison, however, denied all they had said – everything, that is, which could compromise him – and on members of the jury who had been unimpressed by Snelwar, Mintz and Hermilin his sturdy denials may have made some small impression.

He admitted that he had been a regular customer at Snelwar's – though not a daily customer – since the middle of November or thereabouts, and that he had known Beron 'by sight'. But they had never been on friendly terms, he said, for their conversation had been restricted to Beron's 'Comment vous portez-vous?' and his brief reply, 'Très bien.' 'That', he declared, 'was the only communication that passed between us'; and inevitably one suspects that Morrison was minimising their association as, it is probable, the Warsaw regulars had exaggerated it. He told Muir that he had never walked about the streets with Beron, and reminded him that on only one occasion – on New Year's Eve, that is, or early the following morning – had any witness for the prosecution claimed to have seen them together. Sometimes, perhaps, he had sat at the same table with Beron but he had never held Beron's watch in his hand and commented on its weight. Explicitly he denied having spent the whole evening of 31 December with Beron, and recalled the odd fact that Solomon, the dead man's brother, had sworn to having seen Leon, alone in Fieldgate Street, between ten and eleven o'clock: if that were true, it obviously disposed of statements that he and Leon had sat together from supper-time till closing-time. Nor, indeed, had he left the restaurant in company with Leon.

139

There was argument, largely inconclusive, about his purchase of a flute and a revolver; and when Muir asked if he had a gun licence Morrison, with the indignation proper to innocence, replied, 'No, certainly not.' To be in possession of a licence, he implied, was to be guilty of some serious purpose; whereas his only intention was to sell the revolver as soon as he could, and make a little profit on the sale. The evidence of Zaltzman, Taw and Mrs Deitch, that they had seen him in Shoreditch and the Commercial Road, early in the morning of 1 January, he utterly denied, and contemptuously dismissed Nellie Deitch with the words: 'She may have seen me in bed, if she went into my room.'

Never in his life, he said, had he seen Mrs Deitch until she made her appearance at his identification parade; but Muir reminded him of the preliminary hearings at the Police Court, when Mrs Deitch had been asked if Morrison had not taken Eva Flitterman to her house for an immoral purpose. Yes, he had heard that question, said Morrison, but there was no truth in the suggestion: 'I have never been in her house, so far as I know.' It was not he who had instructed his solicitor to make such enquiry, and he could not explain how it had come to be made: 'I cannot tell what is happening in London when I am shut up in prison.' It was, however, at Morrison's request that Abinger had made his damaging attack on Mrs Deitch, to discredit her as a witness, and it seems probable that Morrison knew her better than he was willing to admit.

The story of his alleged visit to the Shoreditch Empire was again repeated, without much addition to it, and then, with a sudden change of direction, Muir asked, 'How long have you known Mrs Frank?' – About eight years, said Morrison. He used to pass the watchmaker's shop, where Frank worked, on his way to see the girl with whom he was then walking out. Mrs Frank used to serve behind the counter of the shop, and they had become acquainted.

'Do you know that Frank is a convicted receiver of stolen jewellery?' asked Muir. He had known nothing of the sort, said Morrison, 'till it was put in the papers after his being cross-examined at the coroner's court'. On Sunday 1 January he had, he admitted, given Mrs Frank ten sovereigns in exchange for two

£5 notes, and, moved by some impulse to dramatic invention, added, 'And I wish to mention to you, sir, that that man has been offered £100 to come forward and give evidence against me.' A detective, name unknown, had made the offer, and Frank had told him of it when he paid a visit to Brixton prison. The assertion, it appears, was not taken very seriously, but Muir asked how often Frank had gone to Brixton.

'Only once,' said Morrison; and then, like some witnesses before him, was tempted to parade his virtue. 'I would not have let him in if I had known what he was,' he declared. 'I did not want him to come to see me, because if I had known what he is I would not have lived in his house.'

Mr Justice Darling's interest was aroused, and he asked, 'Did you think that, if he had been a respectable man, he would have let a room to you, to live with a prostitute in it?' To which Morrison made the remarkable reply, 'There are dozens of respectable men here in London, grocers and all sorts of people, who keep women in their houses.'

'Respectable men?' asked his lordship.

'Quite respectable men – as honest as there can be – at least what I mean is that they have not been convicted of any crime.'

'Is Mr Rotto one of those?' asked Muir.

Rotto, it may be remembered, owned a house in or near Fitzroy Square, to which Morrison, after calling on the Brodskys on 7 January, had taken Jane and remained there with her from about half past seven till ten. Now, when questioned, Morrison said he had known him for seven or eight years, that Rotto had always been kind to him and he was unaware that Rotto had been in custody for receiving stolen goods and was said to be connected with the white-slave trade. All he knew, said Morrison, was that Rotto was a grocer, 'as respectable a man as ever I came across', and 'he has always given me a helping hand'. Rotto, indeed, had found a job for him after he left the Lavender Hill bakery, but he had not stayed because his new employers were Jews, and 'some Jews expect you to work nineteen hours out of every twenty-four'.

His anti-Semitism was strictly limited, however, for Jane Brodsky was a Jewess, and of her he was very fond – he had meant to marry her – and Rotto, another Jew, was his best friend. That was why he had taken Jane to his house.

Returning to the matter of Morrison's activities during the first week of January, Muir asked why he had not returned to the Warsaw, either to eat or hawk his jewellery; and was given the sturdy answer that while Florrie Dellow was cooking his food he had no need to pay fourpence for a tram-ride to Osborn Street. He had, in any case, rarely sold anything at Snelwar's, whose customers were all poor men.

He had read in the papers about the Clapham murder, he said, but a large headline in the *Evening News* of Monday the second – 'The Mad Landlord' – would have meant nothing to him, supposing he had seen it, because the 'landlord' he had known 'was not mad at all; there was nothing the matter with him'. Never, he declared, had he associated the 'landlord' of the Warsaw with the victim of the Clapham murder; after leaving the restaurant he had seen Beron, a few minutes past midnight, in company with a tall, well-dressed man at the corner of Sidney Street; and as to the blood-stains on his collar – if blood-stains they were – his nose had begun to bleed while he was washing under the tap at the back of the Zimmermans' house, and there may have been a little blood on his fingers when he pinned a collar to his shirt.

The Court then adjourned.

III

On Monday 13 March Steinie Morrison was recalled, and Muir resumed his cross-examination. On this, Morrison's third day in the witness-box, there came to light – or, more accurately, into a dim twilight – much of the obscure and tangled story of his early life.

He was asked again if he could produce any letters from the mother in Russia with whom he claimed to have kept up an occasional correspondence, though it seems he was never asked for her address. No, he could not do that, but he could say that her letters, unregistered, had been sent to Steinie Morrison at the General Post Office, London. There were questions about the jewellery he bought and sold, about his little business in gold and banknotes and about visits to a public house called the King's

Head in Commercial Road. In a sweeping statement Morrison disclaimed all knowledge of the King's Head and other such places of resort: 'I never in my life went to a public house, so far as I remember.' Nor, he repeated, had he ever walked the streets with Leon Beron.

Then he was asked who had introduced him to Eva Flitterman in 'a prostitutes' house' in Harding Street. 'The man of the house,' he answered, whose name he did not know.

'Do you know a man named Hugo Pool?' But no, he had never heard of him.

Mr and Mrs Pool were brought into Court, and Morrison admitted that he recognised them, but said they were not the tenants of 2 Harding Street. He had known them for several weeks, since before Christmas, and had called on them at a house in Grove Street which was also 'a prostitutes' house'. He admitted, too – contradicting a previous statement – that on 29 December he had gone to see Hugo Pool at 2 Harding Street, but could not remember if Mrs Pool was there. She might have been in bed, in a room upstairs, but he had never been upstairs. He had spoken to some other women in the house, but he had not asked Hugo Pool to come out and have a drink, 'for the simple reason that I do not drink'.

Then, springing a surprise, Muir asked, 'Was Leon Beron with you in that house on the night of 29 December?'

'Oh, no, certainly not!' But now, it seems, Morrison was a little flustered. He spoke too much, and seemed anxious to cover his tracks. 'He never was with me in any house, so far as I can remember. It is quite possible that he may have visited there. Places like these are visited by all sorts of people. It is quite possible that he was upstairs, because people coming in there generally go upstairs. I have never seen him while I was there on any occasion.'

On that same night, a Thursday, he might have been in the Warsaw, though he could not remember having gone there; but certainly he had not left the restaurant – as Muir suggested – in company with Israel Zaltzman, Beron and an old man known as 'the Colonial'. They might have gone out together, of course, when all the other customers left, but emphatically he denied the rest of the statement that Muir proceeded to read: 'Then Morrison said to Beron, "Come through the Whitechapel Road way." The old man left us and went through Church Lane, and we [Beron, Morrison, and Zaltzman] went down Whitechapel Road to St Mary's Street, where I said good-night and left Morrison and Beron together.' That, said Morrison, is certainly not true. At no time had he and Beron been associated in such a way.

Now Snelwar, on the first day of the trial, swore he had never seen Leon in the company of women, but at the earlier Police Court proceedings David Beron – the brother who was not called to give further evidence – had not substantiated his evidence nor left, on those who listened, the impression that Leon had lived a wholly ascetic life; and if the dead man had been in the habit of visiting brothels he must have had a source of income above and beyond the few shillings a week that he drew in rent from his few poor tenants, and that paid for his board at Snelwar's and his lodging in Jubilee Street. But as to that source there was no enquiry; or none that was reported and has survived.

Then the jury's attention was again directed to the flute which Morrison had bought, as he said, on the morning of 31 December; though against that was Eva Flitterman's assertion – for what it was worth – that she had seen it when she went with him to the Zimmermans' on the twenty-fourth or twenty-fifth. There was argument about the revolver – why, when Morrison left it at a railway cloakroom, did he put the cloakroom ticket under the lining of his hat? – and about the old, tired topic of his arrest and whether Inspector Wensley had or had not said he was wanted for murder. There was further argument about Morrison's mobile habit of life, and frequent change of address; and then his claim to be of Australian birth was questioned.

He replied: 'I am an Australian, born in Sydney, and I have been there eighteen months. Afterwards my people went over to Russia, where I lived for about twelve years. After that I was sent to Germany. In Germany I have been eighteen months. After that eighteen months in France, and from France I came over to England.'*

'When did you come over to England?'

* For comment on this statement see Chapter Fourteen.

144

'I should think it was about 1899 or 1900.'

'What is your name?'

'Steinie Morrison.'

'Is your true name Alexander Petropavloff?'

No, said Morrison, but that was the name he had used when he bought a revolver in Aldgate.

Muir asked him the year of his birth – '1882,' said Morrison; '1879,' said Muir – and suggested he had been born in Korsovsk in the government of Vitebsk in Russia.

That, explained Morrison, was the address he gave when he petitioned the Home Secretary to let him leave England: 'I tried to make out that I was a Russian born, but they would not grant me that petition. As a matter of fact I am not a Russian born at all, but I may be called a Russian, for the simple reason that I was almost a baby when I went there.'

A moment or two later he exclaimed, 'I have had such bad luck here in England.' Throughout his long ordeal, that was his first appeal for pity, and it may have been histrionic. 'Ever since I came to England I have had nothing but trouble, and I tried to better myself for all that. I have done my best to work honestly for my living, until I have been hounded out by these police officers.' Histrionic it was, and Steinie was still fighting: he had not given way to self-pity, he was dramatising his predicament.

Even when Muir insisted that his purpose, when sending his petition to be allowed to leave England, was to deceive the Home Secretary as to the place of his birth, Steinie remained obdurate. 'That account is a true one,' he declared. 'The only thing that is not true is that I was born in Russia. But, as a matter of fact, I am considered a Russian subject in my own country, because I am a baby brought over to Russia.'

Finally, however, after Muir had hammered question after question into him, he admitted that he had given a false name and a false account of his birth to the Home Secretary; because, he said, 'I knew that was the only way they would allow me to leave this country.'

Then Mr Justice Darling intervened to explain to a puzzled jury why Morrison had been disallowed a freedom for which

England was justly famous. 'Were you in prison,' he asked, 'when you sent that petition to the Home Secretary?'

'Yes,' said Morrison.

That question, and that answer, opened the door to a sad and shocking history of crime and punishment; but before it emerged Steinie found opportunity to say that he had never committed a crime before coming to England; that in prison he had adopted a false name, Morris Stein, 'for fear that my relations may discover that I have sunk to the depth of an English prison'; that while he was in prison he had been ashamed to write to his relations, who at that time did not know if he was alive or dead; and he refused to give his mother's precise address – perhaps she did live in Korsovsk in the government of Vitebsk – because he was determined that she should not 'be bothered by you or the police, nor have I any intention to let her know that I am in such grievous trouble'.

A little reluctantly one admits the possibility that he had a mother, still alive in Russia, and willingly one acknowledges that Steinie had an alert, ingenious mind when – with his criminal record about to be exposed – he sees in it a bright, redeeming quality, and demands that it be made known: 'I should wish, since it has come out, that the jury should know what sort of crimes I committed, and see the tools. Among all the tools that were taken away from me there was never in my possession an instrument with which a man could be murdered like this.' A burglar he had been, but never a burglar who used violence in pursuance of his trade.

'When were you first convicted for felony?' asked Muir.

'I cannot say. 1900 or something like that.'

'Was it 17 December 1898?'

'That might have been it.'

'You were nineteen years of age at that time?'

'That is the age I gave.'

'Did you give the name of Moses Tagger?'

'Yes.'

'What did you say your nationality was then?'

'I said a Hebrew, as I know to speak that language as good as English, so I went in as a Hebrew then.'

'Yes, but what countryman?'

'As a Russian.'

'Was that for stealing from your master?'

'I never stole anything. In fact, all the convictions I had were for no crime committed whatever.'

'What were you charged with stealing?'

'I cannot remember.'

'Did you get a month's hard labour?'

'I did.'

'For stealing some ledgers, the property of your master?'

'That is what they made it out, but fancy a man stealing books! What use are they to him?'

A fine, contemptuous indictment of the law and its follies – but it could not prevent Muir from revealing a sentence of six months' hard labour for burglary on 1 August 1899; fifteen months' imprisonment on 15 April 1900, for being in unlawful possession of cigars, pipes and tobacco, the proceeds of a burglary; and on 10 September 1901, five years' penal servitude for burglary. Released on licence in August 1905, Morrison was rearrested a year later and charged with being a suspected person and having housebreaking implements in his possession: that he had admitted, but denied possession of a jemmy. A brace and bit, yes, and a chisel with a blade about four inches long. But 'I never had a jemmy or a bar of iron. I have no use for such things whatever.'

'On that last occasion when you were arrested,' said Muir, 'were the proceeds of three burglaries found in your possession?'

'They were, yes.'

'What do you use a chisel for?'

'To get into a house.'

'In through the window?'

'Through the window.'

'Without waking the inhabitants?'

'Without waking the inhabitants.'

'And out again?'

'As a rule, you know' – and Steinie, in temporary command of the situation, again assumes the role of an instructor dealing with a dull pupil – 'the places I commit burglaries in, the

147

inhabitants of gentlemen's houses generally lived right upstairs. There is nobody down below.'

'But you still have to get in and out without alarming people inside?'

'That is the way, yes,' said Steinie, completing his tutorial, 'but you could not do it in a house in the East End, where people are living in every room.'

Re-examined by Abinger, he was asked, 'Have you ever in your life been convicted of a crime of violence?'

'Never in my life – never had a fight with a man in my life – never done violence.'

'Just briefly: have you ever in your life been convicted of assault?'

'Never.'

'Or charged with assault?'

'I have never been charged with any violence of any kind in my life.'

Muir made no attempt to dispute that statement, and Abinger, with marvellous effrontery, tried to minimise, if not obliterate, a revelation of ten years' criminality under a bland summation of his client's misdeeds. 'You have been convicted,' he asked, 'and you frankly admitted it, of stealing some ledgers and some cigars?'

'Yes,' said Morrison.

'What was the date of your release from the last sentence?'

'17 September 1910.'

A few days later he found employment with Mr Pithers the baker, and after that came to an end he drifted into the idle company that frequented Snelwar's restaurant. From somewhere he got considerable sums of money, and for women showed an insatiable appetite that the grim asceticism of his prison life goes far to explain and excuse. He had three and a half months of liberty; he was able to buy new clothes and dress well. He bought a watch and chain, the luxury of clean linen; he was casually generous to the women he favoured. Then, at the door of the restaurant in Fieldgate Street, Inspector Wensley appeared, and half an hour later Morrison was again in prison. Was he a victim to the fatalism of habit, the apathy of the confirmed criminal? Or was he, in his own mind, assured of his innocence? He had had a week in which to find means of escape, and he had made no attempt to escape.

He had left the bakery on Lavender Hill because, he said, the police had 'hounded him out of it'. That was not endorsed by Pithers, but Pithers may have wished to avoid offending the police as warmly as Morrison was intent on vilifying them. Abinger then took him over some familiar ground – that Wensley, when arresting him, had said he wanted him for murder; that Eva Flitterman pretended to have seen his flute, and heard him play it, on 24 or 25 December – and then asked, 'Is it true or not that you took Jane Brodsky round to Rotto's house for an improper purpose?'

To which Morrison magnanimously replied, 'Jane Brodsky is as innocent a girl as ever there was in this world. She is as pure and innocent a girl as anybody's daughter, and anybody saying against that is a liar.' That the girl had gone upstairs he did not deny: 'Yes, where Mrs Rotto was in the parlour. She was with us all the time.'

Was Morrison speaking the truth, or proclaiming Jane's chastity in order to show that he too could, on occasion, behave virtuously? Members of the jury must have formed their own opinion, but whatever it was it had little relevance to the charge of murder they had to judge.

Then Abinger read, from the *Evening News* of 2 January, two long extracts from the story about the 'Mad Landlord' of the Warsaw Restaurant to which Muir had previously drawn Morrison's attention; and got no useful response. He may have read the article, said Morrison, but it was such a long time ago that he really could not remember. And on that inconclusive note the examination, cross-examination and re-examination of the prisoner at last came to an end.

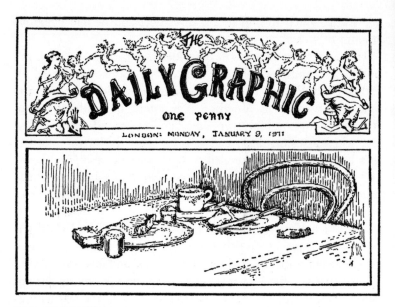

ELEVEN   *The unfinished meal in Cohen's Restaurant*

I

CONTINUING his case for the defence, Abinger struck a familiar
note. If the flute which Morrison had handed for safe-keeping to
Mintz in the Warsaw Restaurant, on the evening of 31 December,
was, in fact, not a flute but an iron bar wrapped up in brown paper,
could that iron bar have been the weapon with which Leon Beron
was battered to death on Clapham Common?

That, in effect, is the sum of the questions that Abinger put to
his next witness, Dr Jonathan Fearnley. He, having seen a photograph of the deceased that showed on the right-hand side of his
forehead a wound of approximately horse-shoe shape, gave his
opinion, for a start, that the injury had been inflicted by a single
blow. His testimony may or may not have been weakened by a
question from his lordship, who asked if he had seen the dead
body. Dr Fearnley admitted that he had not, and with apparently
undiminished confidence described the injury, as revealed in the

photograph, and said, 'I think that an angular instrument, such as a hammer, must have been used.' And in reply to another question from his lordship he added, 'It must have been an instrument having something at the end of it, at an angle.'

He then produced, and handed to the jury, an iron bar one and a half inches in diameter and weighing twelve pounds, and told Abinger that such a weapon could not have caused such an injury as that which he had described. He amplified his reply, and said that even with two blows a straight bar could not have produced the arc-like wound on Beron's forehead. In his opinion, for what it was worth, Beron had probably been knocked down before the lethal blow was struck – such a blow would be likely to glance off a standing figure – and certainly Beron had already lost his bowler hat.

Questioned about the probability, or otherwise, of the murderer's clothing being blood-stained by so violent an assault, Dr Fearnley was professionally cautious, but finally gave Abinger the answer he wanted. 'Assuming', said Abinger, 'there is a quantity of blood upon the coat of the deceased man, particularly about the collar, in your judgment could he have been dragged as I have described to you by his assailant, turned over and arranged, without blood getting upon the sleeve of the assailant's coat?' 'I should expect to find some part of his overcoat, either the sleeve or the skirts in front, or his trousers possibly, smeared or soiled with blood,' said Dr Fearnley.

Copies of the *Daily Chronicle*, the *Daily Mail*, the *Daily Mirror* and the *Daily News*, all dated 10 January, and of several weekly papers dated the seventeenth, were then exhibited, in each of which there was a portrait of Steinie Morrison: it might have been difficult, one feels, to find anyone in London who, at an identification parade, would have failed to pick him out. And in the *Daily Graphic* of 9 January there was a picture of the restaurant in Fieldgate Street over a caption that read: 'The unfinished meal left in Cohen's restaurant, Fieldgate Street, Whitechapel Road, yesterday morning by the man who has been detained in connection with the Clapham Common mystery. He was seated in the empty chair on the right.'

Francis Edmond Bell, assistant art editor of the *Daily Graphic*, testified that 'The first intimation I had of this arrest came by the Exchange Telegraph Company's tape shortly after one o'clock on Sunday, 8 January. In consequence of that tape message the photographer was sent. The written description would not be prepared until it was confirmed from other sources.' To members of the jury it may have seemed that Abinger had been justified in so stubbornly maintaining his assertion that it was Wensley who first spoke of murder when Morrison was abruptly removed from his breakfast-table. Wensley was called on to renew their debate, but before that Mr Pithers the baker made a brief reappearance. He could not confirm Morrison's statement that the police had 'hounded him out' of honest employment, but admitted that on two occasions he had found a uniformed constable in his bake-house, whose business he did not enquire and of which they said nothing. Unwittingly, perhaps, he exposed the difficulties of the life that Morrison's criminal record compelled him to live when he confessed that if he had known of his previous convictions 'I do not think I would have taken him into my employment'. Morrison's only trade, as it seemed, was burglary, but he could scratch a living by hawking cheap jewellery as well as by baking bread. He was, it may be thought, the sort of outcast whom a strongly motivated but cautiously moving club or coterie – clique or *camarilla* – might have decided was safe and serviceable for a single, well-paid job that had to be done; and the club or *camarilla* may have had money to spare.

To Wensley, when he was recalled, Abinger addressed the question: 'Could you have put your finger upon Morrison, if you had wanted to, before 8 January?'

'I could not,' said Wensley. 'I did not know, nor had I heard before 8 January, that he was in Whitechapel.'

'What did you arrest him for on the morning of the eighth?'

'That he, being a convict on licence, failed to notify his change of address.'

'How many police officers did you take with you to effect that arrest?'

'Four besides myself.'

'Do you tell the jury that it is usual to take five officers to detain a man for failing to notify his change of address?'

'If that had stood alone, no.'

Abinger pressed him hard, and from a very tight corner Wensley escaped only by a hardy exercise in sophistry; or, as some may prefer to think, by sheer effrontery. He was asked if, on oath, he would tell the jury that he had not taken Morrison for murder; and he answered, 'I took him for failing to notify his change of address, and with the possibility, as I then knew, of his being charged with murder.' Abinger repeated his question: 'Do you pledge your oath you did not arrest him on suspicion of having committed a murder?' 'Certainly,' said Wensley. 'I have said so over and over again.'

Stubbornly he maintained that on the day of Morrison's arrest the police had still no information to connect him with the murder. He was reminded of Nellie Deitch's statement, on 2 January, in which she swore to having seen Beron, in the early morning of the first, walking with a tall man whose description, as she gave it, fitted Morrison fairly closely; he was reminded of the cabman Castlin's statement on the fourth; of Jack Taw's statement, and several others; he was shown the photograph in the *Daily Graphic* of 9 January, and Abinger asked him how it could have got there – why it should have been published – if he had not said Morrison was wanted for murder. Wensley could answer neither to *how* nor *why*, but still refused to budge from an untenable position.

The case for the defence drew quietly to a conclusion amid the muttering of some minor witnesses – a meteorologist subpoenaed to prove there was no moon on the night of the thirty-first was not heard – and then Muir, to offer further evidence for the prosecution, called Hector Munro, acting manager of the Shoreditch Empire, who demolished Jane Brodsky's story about spending New Year's Eve there, in shilling seats not far from the front and not far from Steinie Morrison. According to Mr Munro the seats in the front rows, from A to I, were for that performance reserved at one and ninepence, and all had been booked by five o'clock. It would have been quite impossible for her and her sister, arriving about nine o'clock, to find vacant seats anywhere in the house: there were 310 seats on the ground floor, and 502 people were admitted.

Muir further attempted to show that Morrison's account of having bought a flute in the High Street, Whitechapel, on the morning of the thirty-first, could not be true because on Saturday morning there was a hay market in the middle of the street, and no stalls were permitted in that part of it where Morrison pretended to have made his purchase. A hay market in Whitechapel may have done something to mitigate the squalor of the neighbourhood, but Abinger objected to it – objected to the evidence of its existence that a police constable was prepared to give – and supported his objection with a very pretty piece of legal trinketry.

Muir, he said, having cross-examined the prisoner upon certain matters 'on a certain issue', was now proceeding to call evidence to controvert the oath of the defendant: 'I submit that he can only do so where the matter that he is cross-examining about is relevant to the issue, and if it is not relevant to the issue he is bound by the defendant's answer.' Debate ensued – what *was* the issue? – and his lordship thought the law had been clarified, the argument settled, in a comparable situation in that notorious case, *The King v. Crippen*. But no, said Abinger, that was entirely different, and offered his own definition of the present dispute.

'The Crown', he said, 'allege that on the night of the murder the prisoner took away from Snelwar's restaurant a parcel containing a bar of iron. On the other hand, the prisoner says on the night of the murder, "I took away a parcel which contained a flute." That is strictly relevant to the issue. Now my learned friend is trying to prove that the prisoner when in the box, swearing that he bought the flute on that day, was not telling the truth; that he bought it at some other date. That is not the issue. The issue is, was this a bar of iron or a flute that the prisoner purchased?'

It was, he admitted, a very difficult question, but his submission was that the constable's evidence about the hay market was not admissible; and his lordship gave him the benefit of the doubt. When, however, his lordship explained that 'There are some things in which one favours a defence, and this is one', Abinger's pride was hurt, his honour offended and he tried to refuse a decision founded on favour. Grandly he declared, 'If it be evidence, let it be admitted.'

154

But his lordship refused to be drawn into further argument, and no more was heard of the Whitechapel hay market.

II

Mr Abinger then rose to address the jury on behalf of the prisoner, and with a measured emotion spoke of the responsibility that lay upon counsel who undertook the defence of a man charged with murder: by his argument members of the jury might be affected for a week, but for the man in the dock its failure could spell eternity.

The prosecution, he said, had made much of the fact that Morrison did not go to the police and tell them he had known the dead man. But Morrison was a convict released on licence, a fact which the jury might never have learnt if his character had not been attacked in cross-examination, and his criminal record exposed – a record that gave him reason enough for avoiding a police station.

It was unwise of Abinger to allude, so early in his speech, to those two witnesses, called for the Crown at the Police Court but not called again, who had retracted their evidence; but he could not forgive Eva Flitterman and the boy Rosen – he could not forget their perjury – and the woman Nellie Deitch was almost as bad. He and Morrison had known the danger invited by questions that impeached her credit and her character, but it was necessary to demonstrate the falsity of some of the witnesses called for the Crown.

The jury, said Abinger, now knew Morrison's history, 'and speaking frankly, I am glad you know it!' By such a statement he may have invited incredulity, for many do not speak truly when they claim to be speaking frankly; but probably he was honest, and assuredly there was feeling in his voice when he said, 'For now I am free, I can say what I like.' And his second, perhaps more cogent reason for relief and gratitude lay in his claim that Mr Muir, his learned friend, had exposed the weakness of his case by making such a parade of Morrison's lamentable past life. If the Crown had had a clear and conclusive case against the prisoner, there would have been no need to dwell upon his shame. The case against him was so weak that it had little chance of acceptance unless his deplorable history was made known, and he was revealed as a criminal. And still, despite exposure, there was no suggestion that he had ever used violence, he had never been accused even of the simple rudeness of common assault. But a jury, of course, could sometimes be persuaded to think more about a prisoner's past than about matters relating to his present plight; and he begged them to remember that danger.

Now, with a quickening intensity, Abinger thrust into view the weaknesses of the case for the prosecution – the omissions in it – and tried to transform them into solid ground on which to build his defensive system. What, he asked, was the motive for the murder? There was no scrap of reliable evidence that Beron had had money in his pockets, and his suggestion was that robbery, as an inducement, could be eliminated. But what motive remained? It was strikingly obvious, said Abinger, that from the moment when he opened his attack Mr Muir had carefully avoided reference to the photographs which showed, on the cheeks of the murdered man, superficial cuts that resembled the letter S. Once and once only had he mentioned them; but the jury must consider their significance.

Leon Beron, living in Jubilee Street, was known to the police, and there was an anarchists' club in Jubilee Street. On 16 December, in Houndsditch, three policemen had been murdered in atrocious circumstances, and all London was ransacked to find the assassins. There were arrests on the twenty-second and twenty-third, but there was no pretence that the ringleaders had been found. 'Peter the Painter' was still at large. Then, on 1 January, Leon Beron was murdered, and two days later, in consequence of information received – so Inspector Wensley had declared – a house in Sidney Street was surrounded, and in the subsequent action two men were burnt to death. But 'Peter the Painter' was still at liberty and when Inspector Wensley was asked 'Who are the other persons you are looking for?' he replied, 'I would rather not answer that question.'

That reply – in the circumstances, no doubt, judicious – Abinger left swinging like a weathercock in the draught of opinion, and brought the jury back to Clapham Common. If robbery had been the murderer's motive, he said, every moment would have been counted, every moment precious. But, in fact, two murderous blows had been dealt to kill Beron, and then precious time was spent on scoring or slashing rough likenesses of the letter 'S' on the dead man's cheeks: the initial letter of the Russian word for 'spy', and also – though this seems to have gone unnoticed – the initial letter of the English word for *espion*, *mouchard* or *pisteur*. In addition to that, more time had been given to arranging, quite deliberately, the dead body in 'an almost natural' position: an action that had no conceivable purpose other than to draw attention to a crime of vengeance.

Rather superfluously he warned the prosecution against any attempt to establish even a remote connexion between Morrison and the Houndsditch murderers; and in reference to Muir's examination of Ernest Lewis, the bank clerk who was asked to identify Morrison's signature, recalled Muir's ill-natured injunction: 'Look at these S's. Are they not open-shaped like the openings in a fiddle?' A grotesque comparison, said Abinger: what Muir suggested was that a man transported by fury, as a murderer must have been, would slash a corpse as casually as he would scrawl his name on a bank receipt, and wantonly leave his signature on his victim's face.

Nothing belonging to Morrison had been found on the Common. That red and black silk handkerchief: to whom did that belong? Not to Morrison, and if it were not Beron's it must have been the property of the murderer or his accomplice. And as to a weapon, the instrument of murder, what chance – if the prisoner were guilty – had the prisoner had of concealing it? There was, indeed, no evidence that the prisoner had been in possession of such a weapon, unless, of course, the statement of Mintz the waiter was accepted as true. Reject that, and the case for the prosecution was derelict. But, let it be noted, a bar of iron was not a thing that a man usually carried about with him, and it was unlikely that a man who was going to commit a murder would take such a weapon and, in the place where his intended victim sat, give it to a waiter to keep for him. It had to be remembered, moreover, that Mintz had been an inmate of Colney Hatch Lunatic Asylum, and was the prisoner to be sent to his death on such evidence as Mintz could offer?

Mintz and Nellie Deitch, Rosen and Eva Flitterman – in Abinger's mind they lived like ghosts in a house haunted by memories of the evil they had done; and he could not exorcise them. The prosecution had made use of perjured witnesses – he dragged in that old dispute, and reinflated it, but patiently, yet again, Mr Justice Darling dealt with it, brought it down to earth and reality – and the Court adjourned.

III

On Tuesday, 14 March, the eighth day of the trial, Abinger resumed his address to the jury and drew attention to what still seems a curious feature of the case for the prosecution. That was the pretence – and much had already been made of it – that after Beron's murder Morrison had disappeared. So far from that being true, he had gone to the Warsaw early on 1 January, spoken briefly to Snelwar and later in the day spent some time in the Flittermans' house, where he cashed a cheque for £4. Then, having left the good Zimmermans, he slept for three or four nights with Florrie Dellow, but on Monday the second was at the Shoreditch Empire with Jane Brodsky. For much of that week he was walking about Whitechapel, he made no attempt to escape, no effort to lie hidden; but he was not arrested until the eighth. Inspector Wensley's assertion that the police had no cause to associate him with the crime on the Common was disingenuous, and so conspicuous a figure could not have escaped observation: there were always policemen in Whitechapel. They knew he was there, but they did nothing; and it may be they were waiting in the hope that he would do something foolish, and so incriminate himself. But he continued to behave in his normal manner, and after procrastinating for a week Inspector Wensley arrested him while he sat eating his breakfast in a restaurant only a few hundred yards from the Warsaw.

Abinger then struck boldly at what he called the bedrock of the case for the Crown. What had induced Beron to go to the loneliness of Clapham Common, where he was murdered? It was unlikely that he had been persuaded by seeing Morrison take a bar of iron from Mintz the waiter. Beron, when he left the restaurant, was certainly neither drugged nor drunk, and no evidence had been brought to show that Morrison had been urging him to undertake an improbable journey. That was a puzzle to which Muir – 'my learned friend' – had made no reference at all; and the assumption that Morrison had invited Beron to take a walk on the Common was without proof. The habitués of the Warsaw insisted that Morrison and Beron had been close companions, but none could report any conversation he had heard between them.

The police, said Abinger, were talking sheer rubbish when they tried to pretend that two minute blood-stains on Morrison's linen – a spot on his collar, another on a shirt-cuff – were evidence of his having committed a violent murder. The police were admirable men, good men and brave, and he was not going to vilify them; but it was absurd to pretend that he who clubbed Beron with an iron weapon, stabbed him five or six times with a dagger, stooped to cut those mysterious signs on his face, could have risen without soiling his coat with blood. There must have been blood all over his clothes. 'Blood, blood, blood!' exclaimed Abinger – and, though emotion may have untuned his voice, it did not dislodge his reason. The man who bludgeoned or stabbed Beron to his death, and dragged and disposed his body into a mockery of resignation – that man must certainly have left the scene of the crime with more blood upon him than a pin's head on his collar, another on his cuff.

Abinger rebuilt the action: a tall man, pulling Beron's body towards the bushes, must have stooped above it, and by stooping have let the skirts of his long coat sweep blood-stained ground. But no blood was found on Morrison's coat, and no weapon had been found. The murderer must have walked away with them – iron bar and dagger both dripping with blood – and how would he carry or conceal them? In the pockets of his coat? But the pockets of Morrison's coat were clean.

If robbery had been the motive that prompted murder, what evidence was there that Morrison had got his profit? That was a question the jury must answer. They must also refrain from condemning him for what he had done in the past: he could not be convicted of murder because he had been convicted of burglary. It would have been different, of course, if he had ever been charged with violent crime. But no such charge had ever been brought against him, and the prosecution could have had only one motive for revealing his criminal record, and that was to excite prejudice against him.

As to the real motive for murder, it could not have been robbery – now Abinger was repeating himself – for no highwayman would pause to wound and disfigure his victim as Beron had been wounded. And where were the proceeds of robbery? The banknotes found in Morrison's possession had all been accounted for, and there was, in fact, no evidence that Beron had ever owned so much money. Beron was a poor man. He was not murdered for his money, said Abinger, but for revenge. His murder was an act of vengeance 'for what he knew in connection with the Houndsditch police murders'.

That was a bold statement, but Abinger made no attempt to define or clarify what part, if any, Beron had played in the search for those mysterious assassins, or their identification. The police said firmly that he had had no association with the Houndsditch crime, but in England a vast number of newspaper-readers would have been deeply gratified if Abinger had been able to establish a link, however tenuous; and members of the jury may have waited expectantly for revelation. But, if such was their mood, they were disappointed, and Abinger again fell victim to emotion – was again unbalanced by that fearful apparition of perjury, dim-witted Eva Flitterman, whom he could not banish from his mind – and absurdly he exclaimed, 'There is a woman living in London; there is a woman walking up and down the corridors of these Courts who is to be found to come here and to invoke the name of the Almighty and swear that she saw this man with a £5 piece – knowing it is a lie – and in a murder trial. It is appalling. You have consciences; we have consciences; has that woman?'

'Mr Abinger,' said his lordship, 'what do you want? Do you want the prosecution to call her or not?'

'No, my lord,' said Abinger, 'I do not want them to call her. It would be a terrible spectacle.'

There is no point, said his lordship, in calling witnesses if you and the prosecution and everybody else know that they are only going to tell lies. Abinger agreed, but then declared, 'I want that woman to be brought into Court so that the jury may see the class of woman she is.'

'What is the use of looking at one liar more or less?' asked his lordship.

'My lord must be thinking of Rosen,' said Abinger. 'Another liar – although, of course, not such a shocking liar as Flitterman, but another liar, the next liar – '

His lordship interrupted to correct him: 'I was thinking of the observation of King David – not of Rosen.'

The jury may well have been puzzled by his lordship's allusion, but Abinger was infuriated. 'I wish I had the remarkable abilities of my lord!' he exclaimed. 'He is able to allow his mind the luxury of dwelling upon King David when we are discussing this sordid case. Gentlemen, of course you know my lord's literary talents: I have none!' And then, finding another topic, he attacks it with the incoherence of a man on the very edge of frenzy. It is the topic of Beron's last supper, of the paper bag that held the crumbs of a ham sandwich.

He addresses the jury: 'You remember the paper bag which was found upon the deceased man. Ward tells Cooper to go there and ascertain what sort of shop it is, and this is what Ward told you Cooper reported: 'It is a sort of refreshment house.' Ward tells us that is not true; it is not a sort of refreshment house at all; it is a pastry-cook shop. Cooper told Ward it was a sort of refreshment house; that would lead you to imagine that you could get sandwiches there. It is a pastry-cook shop where they do not sell sandwiches; they sell arrowroot.'

Mildly his lordship pointed out: 'The fact that they did not in that shop sell sandwiches does not prove that there had not been sandwiches in that paper bag.'

'I agree,' said Abinger.

'There is distinct evidence that there were the remains of sandwiches in that paper bag, and that there was partly digested meat in the stomach of the deceased man.'

'I accept your lordship's correction,' said Abinger, but with, as it seems, a barely suppressed anger continued to berate the policemen, Inspector Ward and Sergeant Cooper, for their failure to distinguish, with sufficient clarity, between the sort of shop where one could go to buy an arrowroot biscuit, and that which purveyed ham sandwiches. He did not dispute the possibility that the deceased had bought sandwiches, but ham sandwiches – for a Russian Jew, and on a Saturday – 'Well, that is rather a large order to swallow. Do you think Beron was the sort of man to go about eating pork sandwiches on a Saturday? I suggest that an arrowroot biscuit is much more likely to have been his last meal of the day.'

The point that Abinger was trying to make was by no means obvious, but gradually it became apparent. His lordship reminded him of certain medical evidence: Dr Needham's *post-mortem* examination had revealed the presence of partially digested meat in the dead man's stomach, and the fact that he might also have eaten a biscuit could not dispose of that sworn testimony. Abinger professed himself obliged to his lordship, who added, perhaps unnecessarily, 'You must not say that the doctor is telling an untruth.'

'My lord does not appreciate my point,' said Abinger. 'My point is that the man had a meat supper. He did not call at a pastry-cook shop and have ham sandwiches, he sat down and had a meat supper. Where, gentlemen? That is the point of these observations. Where? And with whom?'

Abinger was indeed indicating another weakness or *lacuna* in the case for the prosecution. It was Muir's pretence that on the night of the murder Morrison's movements had been plotted and were known except for half an hour – give or take a few minutes – in which the deed of blood was done. But that theory ignored the certain fact that at some time between leaving Snelwar's restaurant and turning to recognise death on Clapham Common Beron had eaten enough to leave a little pap in his stomach, and with it a smell of alcohol. It was, of course, essential to the case that Morrison had stayed with him, but the prosecution had made no attempt to suggest where they ate and drank. Beron was an abstemious man and so – apart from his innocuous liking for cherry brandy – was Morrison: by his own account he never went into a public house, and though there had been evidence enough that he was an open-hearted lecher no rumour of drunkenness, or even of tippling, had come to shock the jury. But – whether Morrison was with him or not – something very unusual, something strange and odd, had happened after Beron left the Warsaw: that man of parsimonious and frugal habit had, after midnight, been persuaded, by someone unknown at an unknown rendezvous, to eat and drink before yielding to undisclosed and undiscoverable argument, and then, with his murderer, walk into a dark emptiness.

Abinger had a point, but made it, not with a rapier, but with a poker. Beron had eaten a sandwich – there was evidence of that – but no evidence that he had sat down to 'a meat supper'. So said that poised and judicious man, Mr Justice Darling. 'If he had a meat supper, as you say, where is it? There is evidence that the remains of sandwiches were found in his pocket; and what occurs to me is, that if he had a meat supper, why did he get given to him, or buy, or take from somebody else, sandwiches?' And, his lordship added, 'there is evidence that somewhere and somehow he got alcohol'.

'That is one way of looking at it,' said Abinger gloomily.

'Those are the simple facts,' said his lordship; but Abinger, having added arrowroot to his obsessions, continued to discuss the contents of paper bags, in which only crumbs had been found, until his lordship sealed the issue by quoting the moving and immediate evidence of Inspector Ward: 'The body was searched. One halfpenny was found upon him. In the right-hand pocket were two paper bags with the remains of ham sandwiches in them. There was very little left, as though a person had eaten sandwiches by breaking them in his pocket.'

Abinger then drew the jury's attention to the fact that, although there were witnesses who testified to having seen Morrison and Beron together on New Year's morning, no one had ever spoken of seeing them together, except in the restaurant, before that sinister date.* He referred, yet again – and simultaneously every member of the jury may have shielded a yawn – to the see-saw question of who, if anyone, had spoken of murder when Morrison was arrested; and harshly declared that 'Now I come to what I consider the real part of the case.' That is to say, the question of identity and of a witness's faculty of identification.

In this matter Abinger had opportunities of which he took solemn advantage. He began by asking, 'How often was a London cabman asked to identify his fare?' He recalled a recent case in

* Abinger was at fault here.

which witnesses, having identified a suspect, realised they had made a mistake, and recanted; and he warned the jury that if they, in the duty that lay upon them, made a comparable error, they might have no such chance to think again: it might be too late. In a case of murder they were entitled to say to the prosecution, 'You must convince us beyond any reasonable doubt of the identity of the person accused.'

There were witnesses, said Abinger, who had done business with Morrison, but felt unable to identify him, when invited to do so, though they had had better opportunities of seeing him clearly than cabmen engaged in the middle of the night. It was five days since the cabmen had given evidence, and Abinger, summarising their story, was justified in sharpening it with a slight edge of cynicism. There was the all-important matter of clocks and time-tables, of journeys by cab and the time they consumed, and in dealing with that matter, he said, he proposed to strike an average between some of the estimated or given times. According to his calculation Hayman, who on 1 January picked up two men at the corner of Sidney Street just before or just after two o'clock, and timed his journey at 45 minutes, would drop his passengers at Lavender Gardens at $2.42\frac{1}{2}$ a.m. Then Stephens, the second cab-man, picked up his fare and drove off at $3.12\frac{1}{2}$ a.m. It was possible, however, that the murderer had had rather more than 30 minutes for his task; perhaps as much as $34\frac{1}{2}$ minutes. Allow 10 minutes from Lavender Gardens to the spot on Clapham Common where the murder was committed, and 11 minutes for walking thence to Clapham Cross – subtract 21 minutes from $34\frac{1}{2}$ – and the maximum time for the act of murder was $13\frac{1}{2}$ minutes, or 9 minutes if Hayman's own timing was accepted. Within that period the murderer had had a lot to do: the act of killing had been pro-tracted, the dead man's clothes were thoroughly searched and everything of value – his watch and chain, whatever money he carried – taken from them. The body was dragged towards the bushes, buttoned up and tidily disposed. Then the murderer had to get rid of a crowbar and a dagger, clean his hands, compose himself and repair his appearance until he was presentable enough to summon a cab at Clapham Cross.

Time lay at the very heart of the case, and how witnesses had been allowed to juggle with it! There was Mrs Deitch who said she had seen Morrison with Beron at about 1.45 on the morning of the murder; but then her timetable had been amended, and it was accepted that she must have seen them after two o'clock. And what were they to think of Hayman's power of observation when, as they knew, Beron wore a coat with a conspicuous astrakhan collar, but Hayman never noticed it, though apparently he was able to give an accurate description of Morrison? Why were Hayman and Castlin both able to remember and describe the prisoner, though neither could say anything of his alleged companion? Were they, in fact, identifying the original of the photograph that everyone had seen in the papers?

On a moonless, cloudy night the cabman Stephens had been able to see his fare so clearly that he could describe him with great particularity; but after telling the police he had picked him up at half-past two he obligingly altered the time to make it fit in with Hayman's evidence. Morrison's photograph had been published in the papers on 9 and 10 January, and it was not until the tenth that Stephens came on the scene to identify him. He did not suggest that Stephens had intended to commit perjury, but what his mind had imagined, his eye had been taught to see. It should be remarked, moreover, that Mrs Deitch had said Morrison was wearing a cap, but it was a billycock when Hayman saw him, still a billycock when Stephens picked him up, but when he accosted Castlin it was a cap again.

'The prisoner's own account', said his lordship, 'was that he was wearing a cap.'

Abinger agreed, and then made the sensational statement that Castlin drove the men who got into his cab at Kennington to Tottenham, 'a hotbed of anarchism'. A man escaping from a scene of murder, he said, would surely be anxious to get home and to bed as soon as possible; but Morrison lived in Newark Street, and if, in Castlin's cab, he went to Seven Sisters Road, he would be farther from home than he was in Clapham. There was no evidence that Morrison – if he were the man in Castlin's taxi – had returned to Newark Street in the early hours of the morning, when Whitechapel was 'full of police, some of whom must have seen him'.

Policemen patrolling Whitechapel, anarchists astir in Tottenham – Abinger, it is clear, was again contemplating, with a new freshet of excitement, the extraordinary background of recent violence, and a mystery that defied explication, against which his client stood in dangerously high relief. The Crown, he told the jury, is asking you to convict the prisoner of murder on circumstantial evidence. But circumstantial evidence must point to one man, and one man alone. Well, was the prisoner the only man on whom suspicion rested, or might be thought to rest?

Was it not possible that Beron had given information to the police about the Houndsditch murderers? He might have been a useful man to employ. When drama moved into Sidney Street, two men were killed in the besieged house they occupied, but 'the arch-fiend, Peter the Painter', was still at large. One can say with certainty that Abinger's knowledge of Peter the Painter was quite insufficient to warrant so startling a title, but it was agreeable to contemporary opinion and reflects a popular view. He was not going to suggest that Peter the Painter had murdered Beron, but did not the facts of the case suggest that vengeance, not robbery, was the motive?

'Just before I sit down, gentlemen' – would the jury respond to flattery? – 'let us have a quiet, intellectual, dispassionate discussion.' Again he defined his theme – that if circumstantial evidence is to be accepted as proof, then all the facts brought out must point in the same direction – but, admirable though his proposition was, it did not promote quiet and dispassionate debate.

In the present case, he suggested, some of the facts might point to a person, other than the prisoner, who had been impelled to murder, not for the sake of profit, but to wreak revenge. 'It must be plainly understood that I am going to make no charge, no insinuation whatever,' he declared; and carefully explained that what he proposed to say would be directed simply to seeing whether circumstance, and the evidence of circumstance, might not be so interpreted as to point to some person not hitherto suspected. 'Take, for instance, Solomon Beron. . . .'

That, as things turned out, was an unfortunate suggestion. Though Abinger went out of his way to warn his learned friend, Mr Muir, against false assumptions – against any notion that he was imputing guilt to Solomon, or had any other purpose than to frame an illustration *ex hypothesi* – his disavowal failed to pacify Solomon, and even in Mr Justice Darling's mind left a little doubt, a small uneasiness.

'Let us see', said Abinger, 'what facts there are to which these observations might apply. The motive? Who would benefit by the death of Leon Beron?'

'Mr Abinger,' said his lordship, 'do I understand that you are proceeding upon the hypothesis that Solomon Beron may have committed this crime?'

'No,' said Abinger, and reiterated his belief that circumstantial evidence in the case was not all directed to Morrison, and Morrison alone, but might equally point to Peter the Painter 'or somebody of that description'.

'I understood', said his lordship, 'that you were going to argue that the facts might just as well point to Solomon Beron.'

That was more than Solomon could stand. It was he who, on the first day of the trial, had described himself as 'an independent gentleman', living at Rowton House on sevenpence a night, and lost his temper when Abinger, rudely and foolishly, asked from where he had got such good clothes. He seems to have been a man of volatile temper and minimal intelligence, but it is possible that he had been frightened out of his wits – what wits he had – by his brother's murder, and the last fretted rein of self-control was broken by the appalling suggestion that he might have been involved in it. In a maniacal temper, raving and gesticulating, he stumbled towards Abinger, tried to grapple with him and had to be carried out, still screaming, and removed to the enforced calm of a lunatic asylum.

The remainder of Abinger's speech for the defence may have received less attention than it deserved; and perhaps he cut it short. Again he was involved in argument with his lordship, but stout-heartedly he insisted that his only reason for exposing the hypothetical vulnerability of Solomon was to illustrate the insufficiency of the evidence that appeared to enclose Morrison in a circumstantial net, but might not enclose him alone.

It cannot be pretended that Abinger had done much to establish Morrison's innocence; and it cannot be denied that he had laboured mightily, and often with success, to demonstrate the weakness of the case for the prosecution, the hole in its story, the gaps in its argument, the frailty of the evidence on which the three cabmen identified a briefly seen passenger as the prisoner in the dock. Abinger had done well by his client, and might have done better if he had not sometimes let emotion cloud his judgment.

He insisted – or so it seems – on sharing with Morrison a tragic conclusion to a case in which the law represented public opinion, and both demanded a victim.

TWELVE

THERE was small likelihood that Muir would let emotion override judgment. A man of grimly handsome aspect, he had already shown himself to be ruthless in cross-examination, and, perhaps more remarkably, indifferent to rebuke from the bench. It is easy to imagine that he was dominated by a sense of duty; and it is no more difficult to suppose that he equated his duty with an obligation to secure a verdict for the Crown.

He opened his final speech for the prosecution – or what he expected to be his final speech – with a remarkable display of rudeness: sheer, deliberate rudeness. Abinger, he said, had again and again suggested that he, counsel for the prosecution, had suppressed facts, picked his witnesses, argued upon untenable bases to obtain a verdict – and, for variation, had 'poured flattery on me for the way in which I have performed my duty, and described me as the soul of honour. Heaven save me', said Muir, 'frrom the compliments of my friend!'

Abinger, not yet resigned to defeat, responded so heartily that the speech became a duet, and then – as his lordship was forced to intervene – it was again enlarged. Abinger, said Muir, had wantonly attacked the dead man. According to him, Beron was known to the police – known as a criminal – but had Abinger ever questioned Inspector Wensley about him? Wensley knew the East End, and had known Beron. There was no foundation for Abinger's suggestion, and what was one to make of a man who boasted 'I am not the person to cast accusations on those who cannot answer, and therefore I do not attack Peter the Painter' – and a moment later asked you to say 'that the evidence here before you points to Solomon Beron as much as it

169

points to the prisoner as the man responsible for his brother's death'!

'I protest!' exclaimed Abinger, and when Muir tried to interrupt, declared 'I am addressing the Court'. He had never, he said, suggested that the dead man was a criminal. He had suggested that Beron might have given information to the police, but he had guarded himself, as much as any counsel could, against imputing a criminal motive to him.

His lordship intervened to clarify what Abinger had said – the jury may have thought it needed clarification – and with great care explained how dangerous it was to say such things. It was, indeed, possible to put forward a tenable hypothesis for the sake of argument: 'It is a perfectly possible thing to do, but it is so near the line that I said – and I repeat it – I thought it very undesirable that such a line should be taken, because it is very difficult to distinguish between what is a real accusation and what is a hypothetical accusation.'

'And I obeyed your lordship,' said Abinger. 'I am not complaining of that at all. My friend may attack me, my lord. If I may say so, I enjoy listening to it. But what I am complaining of is that my friend should be permitted to say that I said of the dead man that he was a criminal.'

Abinger was inclined to worry an argument, as if it were a bone, though little meat remained on it; and at this juncture his lordship was either remarkably patient or frankly inquisitive: 'You did state', he said, 'that Beron was known to the police, and you said that was significant. I did not know what you meant.'

'I suggested that he might have given information to the police, and that is why he was murdered. For revenge.'

His lordship – still patient, still questing – could not approve of so indefinite a suggestion: 'It assumes that he might have given information about something – as I understand it – about some organised society because he had belonged to it himself. There is the "S", you know.'

In his charge to the jury Mr Justice Darling would clearly state that he attached no importance whatever to the S-like wounds scored on Beron's dead cheeks, but in this debate, that

Abinger so stubbornly maintained, he does seem to have wondered, for a moment or two, if they had any relevance: 'There is the "S", you know, which means *spic*, which is "spy".'

Abinger jumped at the opportunity presented to him. 'I am sorry to interrupt my friend, but he has brought it upon himself,' he declared. 'And this is the trend of my reasoning. Leon Beron, living in Jubilee Street near an anarchist club; Leon Beron is known to the police; on the 1 January information is given to the police, and Leon Beron is murdered with an "S" scored on his cheek to indicate revenge. He might have been an informer.'

His lordship made some remark, not clearly audible, and Abinger proudly declared, 'The jury have heard what I said.' His lordship, a little wearily, agreed.

Brusque and down-to-earth, Muir attempted to resume his speech and restore his own concept of sense and direction to proceedings which had manifestly lost coherence. Inspector Wensley, he said, had stated clearly that Leon Beron was in no way connected with the Houndsditch murderers, and had given him no information about them. There was no shred of evidence that he had had any association with the anarchist club in Jubilee Street. But suppose – just suppose he had been murdered for revenge – well, who *were* the Houndsditch murderers? 'Russian burglars!' said Muir triumphantly.

'I object,' said Abinger, and pertinently enquired what evidence there was to justify his friend's statement.

'It is a notorious fact,' said Muir.

Abinger brushed that aside. 'I am addressing his lordship,' he said, 'and I submit there is no evidence before the Court to justify my friend making that statement.' And added gratuitously, 'Your lordship is not trying the Houndsditch murderers.'

His lordship accepted the submission, and mildly remarked, 'I was waiting for an opportunity to call on Mr Muir to tell me what evidence there was.'

Bluffly Muir replied, 'Any facts so notorious that the jury may be presumed to have knowledge of them may be evidence'; and strangely continued – until his lordship intervened – 'Nobody knows what the Houndsditch murderers were – '

Mr Justice Darling had grown tired of the subject. 'I do not think I can hold there is evidence here that they were Russian burglars,' he said; but went on to describe Abinger's objection to the statement – to Muir's assertion that they were – as 'wholly spurious'. Abinger had been allowed considerable freedom to talk about the Sidney Street affair, and mention the names of people who, according to him, were connected with it, 'although there is no evidence that they were'. But his objection had to be noted, and the consequence was that 'You must not say they were Russians or that they were burglars.'

'No,' said Muir; and, relying on an English jury's sound distrust of foreigners, brought argument to an end with the cold reminder, 'Their names, gentlemen, were Fritz Svaars and some other similar-sounding names.'

Abinger made a vain attempt to maintain debate, but was silenced by his lordship, and Muir, with a ponderous assertion of authority, told the jury: 'All I am desiring to point out to you is that if somebody, for motives of revenge, had Leon Beron murdered, you want to look for evidence to see who was the instrument by whom that murder was carried out.' It was not impossible for the prisoner to have been that instrument, though his own belief was that the theory of murder for political motives was false. It was based upon nothing but a few slashes on the face of the dead man, and those slashes were either devoid of meaning or merely signified that he who committed the crime – for plunder – was cunning enough to leave marks upon his victim that might divert attention from his real motive.

It was a shaky choice that he offered, between alternatives that had little to commend either of them, but Muir gave no one time to weigh their weakness, and harshly concluded: 'Having said that, I pass from the topic altogether.'

Then – suitably impressed, as one must hope – the Court adjourned, and on the following morning, the ninth day of the trial, it was Abinger, not Muir, who claimed attention.

II

Not often has a brutal murder prompted such angry and continuous drama as attended the trial of Steinie Morrison. Though Steinie was found guilty of murder, his conviction did nothing to solve the dense and persistent mystery that veiled the death of Leon Beron in a darkness less permeable than the wintry gloom of Clapham Common; and throughout his trial – as if to underline the unanswered questions it provoked – there occurred changes of fortune, blunt contradiction, and such loud assault on the character of witnesses, and the evidence they offered, as would have been more at home on a stage set for melodrama than in the ponderous conventionality of the Old Bailey.

Mr Muir, that redoubtable advocate, had demolished the alibi put forward on Morrison's behalf, to establish his presence at the Shoreditch Empire, on the evening of 31 December, by summoning the assistant manager of the Empire to prove that all the better seats had been booked and occupied before Jane Brodsky and her sister could have gained entrance and seen him there; and now, as it appeared, Mr Abinger – as tenacious in purpose as Muir was formidable by nature – was about to uproot and cast aside one of the contentions most warmly maintained by the prosecution.

The trial, as it seemed, was at long last nearing an end. Muir had begun his closing speech, and following that would come his lordship's conclusive charge to the jury. But now, to the Court's surprise, Abinger asked permission to call further evidence, and to justify his request said, 'If your lordship desires me to do so, I shall mention the nature of that evidence.'

'Oh, no,' said his lordship, 'certainly not! Who is your witness?'

'A police officer,' said Abinger. 'George Greaves, 86 H, Metropolitan Police.'

More than once – most tediously more than once – there had been argument as to whether, when Morrison was arrested at his breakfast-table in Fieldgate Street, Inspector Wensley had mentioned a suspicion of murder as the pretext for his arrest, or whether Morrison, out of his own guilty knowledge, had been the first to enquire if that was the charge on which he was about to be detained. The prosecution had favoured the prisoner's guilty conscience, the defence had preferred to believe in Wensley's untimely disclosure of a charge for which, on that date, there was insufficient evidence. And now, as it seemed, Abinger had found a witness – a policeman on duty that morning – who would swear to the fact that Sergeant Brogden, also on duty at the Leman Street police station, had told Morrison, 'You are brought here on a serious charge: on suspicion of murder.'

Constable Greaves was in the charge room at the police station when Morrison was brought in. According to him, Morrison asked, 'What am I brought here for?' and Brogden made the accusation that the prosecution had so strenuously denied. Morrison, said Greaves, had then replied, 'All I have got to say is this, that it is not the first blunder the police have made.'

Greaves related, in convincing detail, all that had happened so far as he had seen or heard – he did not pretend to remember too much – and then said he had made the statement, to the truth of which he had just sworn, at about 12.30 that morning: half an hour after midnight, that is. In the very early morning of Tuesday, the previous day, he had written to Abinger, and posted his letter about 5.30 a.m. In that letter he gave authority to Morrison's counsel to use it 'if he thought fit in the interests of justice'.

The envelope, exhibited by his lordship, was addressed to Mr Abinger, K.C., marked 'Confidential', and postmarked 'London, E., 8.15 a.m., Mar. 14th' on one side, and 'London, E.C., 10.5 a.m., Mar. 14th' on the other – postal services were more expeditious then than now. It was a long letter, closely packed with detail that amplified the constable's story, and his lordship read it all. Then he made his own contribution, and said: 'When these matters were brought to my notice, without any kind of putting responsibility on anybody else, I ordered that whatever may be the consequences to this officer, or to any other officers, or to anybody at all, all this should be made public in this Court of Justice.'

Greaves continued his evidence, and revealed that he had been sent for, late the previous night, and very early in the morning made a statement in the presence of Sir Melville Macnaghten, Assistant Commissioner of the Criminal Investigation Department, and Mr Abinger. 'Questions were put to me by Mr Abinger, and they were written down by Sir Melville. That examination concluded somewhere about half-past one this morning. Sir Melville read out to me what I had stated, and I signed it.'

Then Muir rose to cross-examine, and Greaves replied to the anticipated questions – questions about his precise memory of the events attendant on Morrison's arrest – with modest assurance, and then declared, 'I first spoke of this conversation that I heard between the accused and Sergeant Brogden to some police officers about two or three days ago. I would rather not mention these officers because I cannot mention them with absolute certainty. I think one of them was 209 H Heiler.'

'Let Heiler be telephoned for,' said his lordship, 'and not be informed by anybody of what this witness has said.'

'I do not object in the least,' said Abinger – and his lordship, openly censorious for the first time, silenced him with the crushing rebuke, 'It is not a question of anybody objecting. I am giving directions as to what is to be done in this investigation. I will have no more discussion on it.'

Muir continued his cross-examination, and Greaves, after admitting to gossip with fellow-constables, said he had spoken about the apparent suppression of evidence to a nightwatchman employed by the Salvation Army, and to 'Lewis Zavitski, a barber's assistant, living at 65 New Road, where I also lodge.'

'What made you speak about it to these people?' asked Muir, and Greaves very reasonably replied, 'One likes to talk some-times to people one lives with, and to officers with whom one works.'

That it was a matter of some importance, he said, had occurred to him about five days before, when he read in the newspapers about 'this point of contention'. He had not taken the customary step of first consulting a superior officer but wrote to Abinger because 'there was no time to go through such formalities', and also he 'did not want to interfere in the matter unless it was absolutely necessary'.

He had, he said, been a policeman for nearly eight years, and admitted to having been removed 'four or five times' from one division to another. That Muir already knew something of Greaves – or had quickly been acquainted with his history – became evident when he enquired if Greaves knew ex-Inspector

Syme; for Syme, dismissed from the police, had been attacking them, and accusing them of giving false evidence, in a newspaper called *P.I.P.* Yes, said Greaves, they had worked together at Scotland Yard, and though he had not seen Syme for the last eight months he had sent him 'about two letters'. But he had not, he said, discussed the Clapham murder with Syme.

Abinger queried the relevance of Syme's character or conduct, but his lordship thought the cross-examination permissible, and Greaves, admitting that he had read a pamphlet by Syme in which the ex-Inspector complained about his dismissal, confessed also that he had been suspended from duty 'for making accusations of generally oppressive conduct on the part of my sergeant which I was unable to prove'. Greaves, in fact, had the sort of record which might induce his superiors to describe him – according to their habit – as a trouble-maker or bloody-minded. It seems, indeed – or so Muir's cross-examination implies – that on the morning of Morrison's arrest he had been reproved by Inspector Wensley.

Muir also established the interesting fact that since the Houndsditch murders Greaves had written to Wensley a considerable number of letters conveying 'statements of what I have heard concerning those murders'. He had, said Greaves, acquired the information he gave Wensley from the people in the house where he was living; and in some of the letters he had made definite accusations against persons whom he named.

With some show of unwillingness he said that his informant was another of the Zavitskis, Charles Lazarus, of unknown kinship to the barber's assistant, and denied all knowledge of whether any arrest, or arrests, had been made in consequence of his information. The last of his letters had been sent about a week before pictures, alleged to be of Peter the Painter, were published in the papers – 'about two months ago, that is' – and he had written no more because a detective, speaking for Wensley, had told him that the correspondence must cease.

Re-examined by Abinger, he declared that his motive in writing as he did had been a sense of duty, and that no inducement had been offered to him by Syme, the Zavitskis or anyone else. His only object, he repeated, was to see that the accused 'might have fair play'. To his knowledge he had never seen Morrison before he was brought into the Leman Street police station, nor did he know anyone connected with him.

A trouble-maker or an obstinate, honest man? Bloody-minded, or merely opinionated and overconfident of his own judgment? It is difficult to know what to make of Greaves, but there is some interest in the fact that during further examination by Abinger he asked permission to make a short statement 'in explanation of the letters which I am alleged to have written about the Houndsditch murders'.

'They were hardly letters,' he said. 'They were rough notes. Soon after the Houndsditch tragedy I happened to hear a great deal about it. It was gossip that I heard – it was not in the papers – and I thought it might afford a clue to Inspector Wensley and be of some use to him, and so I gave him a report of what I had heard. Mr Wensley promised me that he would never let anyone know where he got the information from, or where I got it from. He said, "If you hear any more, write it down on paper, put it in an official envelope, and address it to me." I simply carried those instructions out' – until, that is, Wensley said he had had enough.

His evidence about the events of the morning of Morrison's arrest appeared to receive confirmation when Constable Charles Heiler – whose presence had been commanded by Mr Justice Darling – arrived in Court. Heiler testified that he knew Greaves, and 'last night and the night before' his beat had come near to that of Greaves. Greaves, he said, had asked if he had followed the papers closely. ' "Well, I have seen them," I said. "I have been looking at them every day." So he says, "Do you know what was said about the prisoner – whether he made a statement about a murder before there was anything about it said to him?" I said, "Well, so it says in the papers." He then said to me, "Well, if they say that, I know different, because I was on reserve at the time they brought the prisoner in. They told him to sit down. He did not sit down, he came to the desk, and when told to sit down again he said "All I want to know is what I am being detained for." He was then told by one of the C.I.D. officers that he was wanted on a very serious charge – on suspicion of murder. It

G

was then that Morrison said, "You have made some blunders, but no blunder as big as this", or something to that effect.'

Heiler could remember no more of Greaves' conversation, and Muir asked no further questions. Abinger, entitled to comment on the new evidence offered by the two policemen, made no better use of his privilege than to express, disingenuously, his surprise at Muir's failure to recall Sergeant Brogden; who, of course, could have done no more than contradict Greaves and be contradicted by him. It was left to his lordship to sum up the value of what had been said, by either side, on the threadbare topic of who said what on the morning of Morrison's arrest, and from the cold precision with which he reduced a long argument to its inherent insignificance it may be inferred that he was heartily sick of it, and determined to let both Muir and Abinger know what he felt.

Then the foreman of the jury wanted to have a word, but 'No, no,' said his lordship, and permitted himself the luxury of freezing rebuke into an epigram: 'Juries should never express any opinion except by their verdict.'

III

After that interruption Muir resumed his closing speech for the Crown, and informed the jury – who may or may not have believed him – that those responsible for the prosecution had already decided that the issue of which his lordship had just spoken was of no importance, and that it must not influence any verdict 'unfavourable to the prisoner' that the jury might deliver.

He then attempted to assess Morrison's financial resources, and reached a conclusion curiously at odds with his original assumption that Morrison, immediately after Beron's death, was in funds because he had robbed the dead man of the substantial sum he was supposed to carry. Now, adding up the money that Morrison pretended to have received from his mother, his alleged profit from a gaming-table, the few pounds he had saved as a baker – and subtracting what he had spent on clothes – he calculated that if Morrison were speaking the truth he must have had some £44 left; and dramatically asked, 'What's become of it?' His conclusion, and that a lame one, was that 'you have only to examine those figures to see that the prisoner's account of his finances is a false account'.

'It is not a false account,' declared Morrison. 'I can give a proper account, but I have never been asked.'

Abinger interposed his own arithmetic, and from his lordship invited the question, 'Are you addressing me or the jury?'

'Your lordship,' said Abinger.

'But you were looking straight at the jury. I can hear you better if you will turn towards me.'

The arithmetical argument was continued, with no larger conclusion than a reiteration that Morrison's accountancy could not be trusted – a conclusion at which the jury might have arrived long since – and then there was debate, as otiose, about the events, or non-events, at the Shoreditch Empire.

It was with much greater effect that Muir advised the jury to think about the Zimmermans' front door: that door, opening on Newark Street, which was secured by a bolt that shrieked so loudly, when it was used, that everyone in the house was wakened by it. 'Why does that bolt shriek?' asked Muir. And boldly declared, 'Because it has never been used.'

A house where children lived, and tried to sleep; a bolt that could be silenced with a little oil or grease. Is it conceivable that that bolt was habitually in use, and was it likely that a house so protected would be chosen by the prisoner for a lodging? A man whose profession, whose business, whose calling was that of a burglar! The story goes, said Muir, that his landlord or landlady waited up for him every night, until he came home, and then fastened him in with a shrieking bolt that he could not undo without waking everyone in the house and the house next door.

Abinger objected. 'Is my friend', he demanded, 'endeavouring to suggest that my client is a professional burglar? Is my friend entitled to suggest to the jury that this man is carrying on the business of a burglar, without any evidence whatever?'

'He has proved', said his lordship, 'that this man was twice convicted of burglary.'

'Three times,' said Muir.

'He has been twice sentenced to penal servitude for the crime of burglary,' said his lordship, 'and it is proved that he came out on 17 September, and he is on ticket of leave.'

Abinger still protested against the relevance of Muir's suggestion, and his lordship placated him – or, at the least, silenced him – by saying, perhaps with a certain chill in his voice, 'There is no evidence that he was at this time committing burglaries. But Mr Muir is perfectly entitled to make the suggestion that the man was a burglar by profession, and that he was living in this place. He cannot point to any definite burglary that he was then committing, and he does not attempt to do so.'

'In my view,' said Muir, and there was no doubt about the coldness in his voice, 'the last place in the world that would be selected by the prisoner as a lodging, if everything that Mrs Zimmerman says is true, and everything that Mr Zimmerman says is true, would be that house.'

He found occasion to continue his harsh criticism of Abinger, whose closing speech he had described as a 'catalogue of trivialities'; and again accused him of alternating meaningless compliments and 'poisonous suggestions' that the case for the prosecution had been misconducted. It had been proved, he maintained, that Morrison was on intimate terms with Beron, and Morrison had not proved where he bought his flute: the flute, it seemed, was at last admitted to be a flute and not a bar of iron, for Muir now suggested that the fatal weapon was a burglar's jemmy. He spoke of the 'wanton, wicked attack' that had been made on the virtuous Mrs Deitch; and, blaming the newspapers for an excessive interest in the case, showed his anger at the interference suffered by 'detective officers who had been dogged night and day by those bloodhounds of the press'.

Then – but now tediously, and, one imagines, with little effect on ears and minds dulled by repetition – he turned again to the cabmen's evidence of identification. Abinger contradicted him, his lordship again had to intervene and Muir's closing speech came to an end in unresolved altercation. The cabmen's evidence may have been crucial, but only those who valued opinion above evidence of a harder sort can have thought it convincing.

Mr Justice Darling

THIRTEEN

MR JUSTICE DARLING'S charge to the jury deserves its own chapter. Even a summary of it will entail repetition of much that was said during the trial – of some things that have been written here – but the story of the trial, and those engaged in it, claims a deeper interest, in all respects but one, than the brutal drama enacted on the Common, and has to be told to the end. There is in it no central, dominating, unresolved mystery, and the tale of murder has an exasperating, elemental appeal which the trial for murder cannot match; but on other levels the trial is the better tale.

There is the nine days' duel between able, ingenious and recurrently very angry counsel: men of strongly contrasting temper, one passionate in advocacy, the other harsh and obdurate. There is the little crowd of witnesses, emerging from malodorous tenements and the dubious comfort of Snelwar's restaurant: poor foreigners who maintain their tribal loyalties and tell their lies with total resolution. There are the police who serve their cause – and the great public cause of law and order – with Spartan fidelity; and the cabmen whose memory can be called to order. There is the tall, dominating, enigmatic figure of Steinie himself; and above them, remote in his own distinction and the eminence of his gifts, the Judge who was often unable to impose his discipline upon the Court and failed, at last, to convince a stubborn jury that his judgment was better than theirs.

Of Mr Justice Darling the *Dictionary of National Biography* says coldly, 'Not a profound lawyer', but adds, a little more kindly, that he was 'interested in life and human beings, and had sound common sense'. He also had an established status as a wit, but in common with many whose wit was provoked by local circumstance and the challenge of instant opportunity his witticisms have lost their original bloom. He had read widely, and with obvious appreciation, in the literature of England and France; he was a classical scholar who had no Greek; he wrote, in the fashion of his time, occasional verse and prose of a social elegance. In trials of no great moment he did not stand upon his dignity, but allowed much latitude to witnesses and often excited laughter. But in trials for murder his gravity and good intention were admitted by even the least friendly of his critics.

As a small and weakly child he had avoided the Victorian sternness of a public education, and against the common trials and normal difficulties of life he had been cushioned by the generosity of a rich, elderly cousin. It was, perhaps, because of such favour, and the light-hearted cleverness of his verse-writing, that when, before he was fifty, he became a Judge in 1897 his elevation roused great resentment and prompted a leader in *The Times* in which it was bluntly said that although he was a man of 'acute intelligence and considerable literary power', he showed 'no sign of legal eminence'.* He survived criticism, however, and lived to become a national legend, guarded by popular affection and rewarded by the ever-growing esteem of his own profession. As Viscount Hailsham, Lord Chancellor of Great Britain, wrote in 1938: 'He was a kindly gentleman, a lover of England and the life and pursuits of the English countryside,

* Quoted by Derek Walker-Smith, *The Life of Lord Darling* (1938).

with a wide general culture, great industry, complete impartiality on the Bench, a dignified bearing, and a perfect control both of his temper and himself.'*

Add to that an appearance of delicate but precise assurance – a small but incisive dignity, a quizzical eye – and he becomes clearly visible as an elegant outsider at a trial which stank of Whitechapel, sometimes degenerated into a brawl and from an oppressively sordid background found occasional relief in hysteria. It was an ordeal deeply offensive to his fastidious spirit, but he survived it with temper unflawed, composure unruffled, even when the jury ignored the instruction implicit in his charge.

A man of foreign nationality, he said, was being tried for the murder of another man of foreign nationality. 'I know not how in his own country he might be tried, but you will try him, of course, strictly according to the law of England, which, if it differs from the law of other civilised countries, errs always on the side of mercy. It requires more proof, it certainly gives greater advantages to an accused person, and it requires this, that in order to get a conviction you should be satisfied of the guilt of the accused beyond reasonable doubt.'

The jury had heard a great deal of evidence – 'You have heard every point put and put again' – and a great deal of argument. But certain facts were undisputed and indisputable. A man had been killed, and his death was due to murder: 'If you can ascertain who killed him, that person is guilty of the wilful murder of Leon Beron.' Beron had suffered many wounds, his skull had been fractured, he had been stabbed in the body. 'It may be that he was killed by one man only, but it is quite possible that more than one man was engaged. Two weapons undoubtedly were used.'

The blunt weapon, said his lordship, may have been used by a different man from the man who did the stabbing. 'If Leon Beron was the man who was driven by Hayman to the top of Lavender Hill with one man only, whether it was the prisoner or somebody else, then they were joined by another man, or the other man was waiting on Clapham Common. Now, gentlemen,

* Quoted in Walker-Smith.

whether there were two or not two men we do not know, but if two men were employed upon that murder, either the other man was waiting there, if the prisoner was the man who went with Leon Beron in the cab; or, if the other man went with him, Beron did not go with the prisoner in the cab.'

Beyond that, they were in the dark. There was the best of reasons for supposing that Beron had been robbed, and robbery may well have entered into the motive for murder. But it may not have been the only motive: 'There may have been other reasons for killing Leon Beron of which we know absolutely nothing.' It had been suggested that the murder was the work of some secret society, but about the alleged evidence for that – the cuts on the dead man's face – his lordship would not offer an opinion except to say that 'anyone who sees the figure "S" in either of those scratches has either better eyes or a more vivid imagination than I can possibly claim to possess'.

That Beron had been seen, on that last Saturday night, at the corner of Sidney Street at about 11.50 could be accepted as fact: the evidence of Snelwar's customers was substantiated by the prisoner. About the customers' allegations that Morrison and Beron had spent the evening together, and the contradictory story that Morrison had gone to the Shoreditch Empire, his lordship proposed to say nothing, because everything that could possibly be said had been said either by Mr Muir or Mr Abinger. But Morrison and Beron were certainly together at ten minutes before midnight – and where did they go after that? Morrison says he went home, and went to bed; and the witnesses Zaltzman, Taw and Weissberg say they saw the two of them, still in the streets, when it was nearly two o'clock in the morning; and Mrs Deitch, though vague about the time, says much the same thing. If they can be believed, the alibi offered by the Zimmermans does not exist. But is the evidence of Zaltzman and the others convincing? Are members of the jury satisfied that the man they saw with Beron was Morrison, or was it some unknown person? The prisoner may have been lying, and the Zimmermans may have been genuinely mistaken or lying too.

After leaving the restaurant Beron had something to eat – apparently ham sandwiches – and something to drink. But where

184

he got them no one knows. No one has suggested that he took away drink and sandwiches from the restaurant, and no witness for the prosecution claims to have seen Morrison go with him into a place where refreshments could be bought. But somehow or other Beron both ate and drank.

The next thing known – 'I suppose we know for certain,' said his lordship – is that at two o'clock a man hailed Hayman the cabman near the Mile End corner of Sidney Street, and Hayman believes that man to have been the prisoner. Two men got into the hansom, the other of whom, according to the prosecution, was Beron. That is probable – for it seems unlikely that Beron walked to Clapham Common – but not certain, for Hayman does not identify Beron as positively as he identifies Morrison. But Hayman drove two people to Lavender Hill by Lavender Gardens, arriving there – according to calculation – about twenty minutes to three. Members of the jury had also gone there, walked to the spot where murder was done and back to Clapham Cross. They knew, from their own experience, that the murderer had very little time to do what he did, if, as Stephens said, it was about three o'clock when the prisoner got into his cab. 'That is one of the reasons', said his lordship, 'why I suggest to you that perhaps the hypothesis that only one man did it is not the true hypothesis, and why I suggest to you that the fact that two weapons were used to bring about the man's death may well point to there having been two men present, differently armed.'

Then, with scrupulous care, his lordship reviewed the evidence of Stephens and Castlin, and told the jury: 'At this point it becomes very necessary to ask yourselves are you satisfied beyond reasonable doubt – not on the balance of probabilities: that is not it – are you satisfied beyond reasonable doubt that that is the man who was in Hayman's cab, in Stephens' cab, and in Castlin's cab on that night?' 'With what certainty', he asked, 'could you swear to a man whom you saw on a night like that, by the kind of light that there was at those places?' And from there to the newspapers, the photographs of Morrison that they published and the unintended help they may have given to witnesses summoned to identify him: 'I think it is to be deeply regretted that those photographs of the prisoner were published when he was merely an accused person on remand on suspicion of having committed this crime.'

The small spots of blood on the prisoner's clothing should not be accepted as evidence of guilt, he suggested; and commended Abinger's remark that, if Morrison was indeed the man whom Castlin had driven to Seven Sisters Road, it was curious that no one had seen him returning to the Zimmermans' house in Newark Street. Nevertheless, the evidence for the defence left much to be explained. Morrison had done some things which gravely damaged his case. 'But there, again, you must not let that prejudice you. . . . The fact that a man calls a false alibi, calls false witnesses, does not necessarily or by a long way prove that he is guilty.'

Morrison was a foreigner, as were many of the witnesses called. 'Ask yourselves,' said his lordship, 'do you or do you not know that it is very common among people of certain classes and of certain nationalities if they have got a good case not to rest upon that good case? If you have ever talked to anybody who has administered justice in India you will know that there, if they have got a good case, they are not content to rest upon that good case because they are convinced that perjured evidence will be brought against them, and in order to overthrow that evidence they themselves procure perjured evidence to defeat the case which will be made by the other side. Gentlemen, I make that observation, as you see, in favour of the prisoner, to suggest to you this, that if you come to the conclusion that an alibi is false, you should not judge it as strictly against him as if it had been produced by an Englishman; because if you know that there is that habit and that likelihood where foreigners are engaged, you are bound to give him the benefit of every doubt.'

A judge might find it hard to speak with such bland assurance today, but insularity should not be condemned when its native voice is so generous – and a moment later the jury were reminded of legal practice in Scotland, where 'there is the power of giving another verdict besides that of "guilty "or "not guilty". It is possible in Scotland to return a verdict of "Not proven". An English jury cannot do that, but for all that, if they come to the conclusion that the case is not proven, although they may not

186

say "Not proven" aloud in Court, they give what is after all an equivalent verdict. If it is "Not proven" they must not say, "Oh, it is not proven but we find him guilty." They must say, "It is not proven therefore we acquit him." '

Hardly could his lordship have made his own feeling clearer; and with that warning – and a little amplification of it – he was about to conclude his charge when Muir reminded him that he had spoken earlier of his intention to say something of Morrison's criminal record. His lordship repaired the omission, and added carefully that what he had just told the jury 'must not be allowed to prejudice or warp your judgment'.

It is manifest – beyond reasonable doubt – that in Mr Justice Darling's opinion there was insufficient evidence to convict Morrison of the murder of which he was accused; but the jury, retiring at eight o'clock, returned thirty-five minutes later with a verdict of guilty.

Said the Deputy Clerk of the Court, 'Steinie Morrison, you stand convicted of wilful murder. Have you anything to say for yourself why the Court should not give you judgment of death according to law?'

'I've got a great deal to say,' replied Steinie. 'For one matter, the evidence against me as to the funds which has been seen on me on 1 January being the proceeds of the murder. I can prove that in November I had a sum of £300, and out of this £300 I have still got £220. If I can prove that, will that in any way alter the jury's verdict?'

Ignoring the question, his lordship spoke briefly of the 'long, careful, and most patient investigation' that had preceded the jury's verdict. Though the prisoner's case had been supported by evidence demonstrably false, he felt sure that 'that did not unduly weigh with the jury, and that they have convicted you upon the strength of the evidence for the prosecution, and upon that alone'. He did not say that he agreed with the verdict, but moved on to his sombre conclusion. 'As to anything you may have to say for yourself hereafter, you must be advised by your solicitor and your learned counsel. I can say nothing. My one duty is to pass the judgment which the law awards; it is that you be taken hence to the prison from whence you came; that you

187

be taken thence to a place of lawful execution; that you be there hanged by the neck until your body is dead, and may the Lord have mercy on your soul.'

'I decline such mercy,' shouted Steinie. 'I do not believe there is a God in Heaven either!'

FOURTEEN

I

IN 1911 *The Times* had still some claim to its popular byname, 'The Thunderer', and on 16 March a leading article said of Morrison:

> Justice has overtaken him at last, and the country will be rid of a cold-blooded assassin and a most undesirable alien. The case against him proved to be overwhelming. . . . In the mind of the public at large the story of this long trial will confirm very strongly the impression so prevalent of late – that the East End of London counts among its population a large number of very dangerous, very reckless, and very noxious people, chiefly immigrants from the Eastern and South-Eastern countries of Europe. The second impression will be that these people add to the difficulties of the situation by their extreme untrustworthiness, since lying, especially in the witness-box, appears to be their natural language.

The Times, it may be assumed, reflected public opinion, but lawyers must have noted that in passing sentence Mr Justice Darling pointedly refrained from expressing agreement with the jury's finding. The case then went to the Court of Criminal Appeal where the judges, without hearing counsel for the Crown, held that the verdict must stand. Fletcher Moulton adds the illuminating comment: 'There was ample evidence before the jury to justify a conviction, though this evidence was contradicted by that of other witnesses, and in such cases it is for the jury, and for the jury alone, to decide. Even if every member of the Court had been of opinion that he personally would have acquitted the prisoner (and possibly such opinion might be inferred from their judgment), the Court must yet have upheld the conviction, unless they were of opinion that the verdict was so perverse that no reasonable jury would have given it.'*

A petition for reprieve was presented to Mr Winston Churchill, the Home Secretary, who exercised his power of mercy, and the death sentence was commuted to one of penal servitude for life. In some later year Lord Darling – as he then was – said, 'I have no doubt that the Home Secretary was influenced considerably in his decision to order a reprieve by the terms of my summing up.'†
Churchill, more perceptive than the jury, discerned the 'reasonable doubt' to which twelve men and most of England were wilfully blind, and being aware that the essential mystery was still unresolved – that no one knew why Leon Beron had been killed – he may well have thought that testimony unavailable at the time of the trial might still emerge. If that is so, he showed, as some may think, remarkable prescience.

Notice of the reprieve was published on 12 April, and on the same day an English lady, living in Paris, made on oath a remarkable statement that Fletcher Moulton prints as an appendix to his account of the trial. She told the story of a conversation between three men, overheard by her on a tram that she boarded in the Avenue Kléber between the Trocadéro and the Arc de Triomphe. One of the men was a French Jew, short and fat and bearded, who wore an old-fashioned bowler hat with a wide curly brim; there was a second Frenchman, who spoke English very badly; and the third was a tall, good-looking, well-manicured 'foreigner' – so the lady called him – who spoke fluent cockney English with a 'foreign' accent.

The lady, identified only as Mrs M. A. R., was reading a French paper when her attention was attracted by the second man saying, in French, 'What are you doing in the affair Stinie Morrison?'

'Hush,' said the foreigner. 'Speak English.'

'All right,' said the Frenchman. 'Are you going to do anything?'

'No. Gort's (or Cort's) life is more valuable to us than his.'

'Yes, but we cannot let him hang. Can't you write a letter?'

* *Trial of Steinie Morrison*, ed. Fletcher Moulton (1922), p. xxv.
† Walker-Smith, *Life of Lord Darling*.

'That is no good, we did that before.'

'When?'

'In 1907.'

'That wasn't so serious,' said the Frenchman. 'They didn't hang him, they will this man.'

'Well, I'm not going to interfere,'said the foreigner. 'I'm not going to get the police on to me. We can't spare Gort.'

There was further reference to Gort or Cort – insistence on his usefulness – and other conversation of no apparent relevance. The observant Mrs M. A. R. watched the second man get off the tram at the rue de Rome, the foreigner at the rue Tronchet. She followed him to the Opéra and into the Opéra-Pantin tram, which he left at the Boulevard Magenta. Still pursued by Mrs M. A. R. he walked down the Faubourg St Denis, into the rue des Deux Gares and disappeared into the Hotel d'Amiens.

Mrs M. A. R. – who boarded the tram at a quarter past ten in the morning – had not been reading reports of the trial, but she knew the name Steinie Morrison, and something of what had happened to him. She sent her statement to Mr Lane, director of the Paris edition of the *Daily Mail*, who forwarded it to the Commissioner of Police in London; who decided to take no action. The French police failed to find the three men or identify 'Gort', but according to Fletcher Moulton they recognised other names that Mrs M. A. R. had overheard 'as those of members of a well known international gang'.

In 1912 a woman referred to by Fletcher Moulton as 'Mrs X', who was living in Whitechapel at the time of the murder – and was, apparently, still alive in 1922 – told the solicitors who had undertaken Morrison's defence that on the night of the murder 'X' – presumably her husband – had gone out about eleven o'clock, and she had not seen him again for three days. When he came home his shirt was covered with blood, and he burnt it. He threatened to kill Mrs X if she spoke of what had happened, was very agitated when he heard of Morrison's arrest, but apparently found comfort in telling himself, 'There's nothing like a Jew-boy for keeping his mouth shut.'

At some later date, says Fletcher Moulton, Mrs X made a further statement to the authorities that altered entirely the purport of her previous evidence – if evidence it could be called – for now she declared that Morrison had brought Leon Beron to see X, not long before the murder, and the three of them had gone out together. Then, on the night of 31 December, Morrison had called for X at eleven o'clock – and X did not return until three days later.

These clues, if clues they were, were not neglected. Morrison's solicitors, and Abinger too, 'worked unsparingly to obtain their client's release', says Moulton, 'but no tangible evidence to shake the verdict could be obtained'. Neither Mrs M. A. R. nor Mrs X laid a trail that others were able to follow and uncover the truth that may or may not have lain somewhere on its course, or beyond it; but one story suggests that the motive for murder was something larger than Leon Beron's watch and chain, and the other that more than one man had a hand in it.

Steinie Morrison showed no gratitude for his reprieve, no pleasure in the grey confinement of life within the walls of Wandsworth Gaol. Gloomy and embittered, sometimes violent, he continued to assert his innocence, and is said to have sought a return to his original sentence, and the mercy of death. In the end, after ten years of prison, at first in Wandsworth, then at Parkhurst, he found that mercy – not indeed by his own hands – but of his own volition. To so tall and strong a man death did not come easily, but by long fasting he wore strength down, and died at last of wilful starvation on 24 January 1921.

II

Does the manner of his death do anything to substantiate his continued assertion of innocence?

It must be noted that Mr Justice Darling had no doubt of Morrison's guilt, though he was firm in his belief that there had been insufficient evidence to prove it. But Darling's notion of guilt may have been very different from Morrison's. Darling knew the law of England; it is doubtful that Morrison did. If Morrison had been accessory to the murder of Leon Beron, then in Darling's opinion he was guilty of that murder; but Morrison may have believed – and probably did – that only they who were present at the scene of death, and struck the fatal blows, could be called guilty.

If he was not present when Beron died, he had played no physical or violent part in his killing, and therefore thought himself innocent: that was why, in the first week of January when he had had every opportunity and the means to leave London, he had made no attempt to escape. He had 'stood his ground', as Abinger said, because he saw no reason for leaving it.

The weakness of the case for the prosecution was most obvious in Muir's attempts to prove that Morrison was the actual assassin. The motive of plunder was clearly insufficient, for there was no real evidence that Beron carried a substantial sum of money, and it would have been dangerous to pawn that much advertised watch and chain. The watch was never seen again, the killing-weapons vanished and even Muir appears to have conceded that the bar of iron, deposited in the restaurant, was in fact a flute. The pin-spots of blood on Morrison's collar and cuffs were no evidence of his having committed a violent murder, but the absence of blood on his coat and trousers can be accepted as reasonable evidence that he had no immediate part in it. The cabmen's testimony stood wide open to doubt – that is a kindly assessment of it – and how Morrison made his way back to Newark Street, from Seven Sisters Road, remained unexplained.

If, however, one accepts, as a fact, that Morrison had no hand in the assassination of Beron, but in some way was an accessory to it, and an associate of his assassins, then the case against him at once becomes darker and more serious. Sceptical though one may be of the veracity of Snelwar and his customers – of all the sad and angry, defeated but still self-assertive habitués of the Warsaw Restaurant – it is difficult to ignore the unanimity of their evidence that Morrison and Beron had become close friends. Morrison himself commands no belief when he says that they never exchanged words more friendly or significant than 'Comment vous portez-vous?' and 'Très bien'. That lacks all verisimilitude, but the picture of 'the landlord' sharing a table with a newcomer to the Warsaw, in appearance the most distinguished of its customers, and in character perhaps the most engaging – that does carry conviction. Morrison's attempt, moreover, to prove that he spent much of the evening of the thirty-first, not in the restaurant but at the Shoreditch Empire, was utterly discredited; and the obvious fact that he had a reason for denying companionship with Beron, on Beron's last night of life, prompts a suspicion of his guilt – guilt in Darling's definition of it – that cannot be erased. Nor can it be disputed – since Morrison himself admitted it – that he and Beron were together some ten minutes before midnight.

That Morrison had money – far more money than he could have earned as a baker's assistant or a pedlar of cheap jewellery – is also beyond dispute; the question with the insistent question-mark is, where did he get it? That his mother, living in Russia, sent him sums of £20 and £15, in English banknotes, appears to be a story beyond the last elasticity of belief, and somewhere in my narrative I dismissed it as patently a lie. I cannot, however, remove a sliver of doubt and the faint admission that Steinie may have been telling the truth when he claimed to have been born in Australia, taken home to Russia at the age of eighteen months, and then, when he was thirteen or fourteen, sent to Germany for a year or two, to France for another year or more and to have come to England in 1899 or 1900. Was he, in fact, the son of res-pectable parents who tried to give him a liberal, European educa-tion, and whom he disappointed because he was a natural delin-quent, a real bad lot – *mauvais sujet* is the label he might have preferred – who sought refuge in England? He made much of the fact that he had not written to his parents when he was in trouble, because he was ashamed to tell them he had been sent to prison; and even so fluent a liar as Steinie may sometimes deviate into truth.

It is not impossible that his parents were well-to-do, respect-able people, living in the Government of Vitebsk in Russia, who had fled to Australia from local unrest or hostility, and a few years later, having found opportunity for safe return, sought to emancipate their son by education abroad. They would not be the only people whose children disappointed them, and such a background might account for Steinie's tall, superior physique, his distinguished appearance, his extravagance when he had money to spend, his preference for clean linen and his mother's ability to send him English banknotes. If there is any substance in that imagined background, the possibility must be admitted –

small and unlikely though it is – that Steinie was wholly innocent of the crime for which he had been condemned to death.

It is not a possibility that commands acceptance. As the source of his sudden affluence, after coming out of prison in September, a kindly, well-to-do, long-suffering mother in Vitebsk is not eminently plausible or instantly credible. But the possibility, remote though it is, and the explanation, improbable though it seems, cannot be excluded.

More credible, however – far more credible – is the chance that Steinie, soon after leaving prison, met people who, being charged with a mission of criminal intent, saw in him a useful agent for a dangerous task. Who those people were we do not know, and in 1911 the Metropolitan Police may have had no certain knowledge of them. But Steinie was a man with a criminal record who would find it difficult, if not impossible, to earn an honest living, even if that were his hope or intention. He was a man of commanding presence, ready and quick in speech, with no discernible morality other than a natural disinclination to violence and brutal behaviour. But what his new associates wanted him to do would not entail violence. They wanted him to make friends with a man of mysterious antecedents – mysterious to us in our age, that is – who lived in Whitechapel and was apparently possessed only of a meagre income that let him live very frugally on a few shillings a week. That man, however, enjoyed a local reputation for wealth exceeding the known sources of his income, and in his own circle was called 'the landlord'. In his own circle it was believed that he had some sort of claim to a handsome but inaccessible fortune; and it seems likely, indeed, that he was supplied with funds – not necessarily large – from a source other than the few small houses whose rents he drew.

Now 'the landlord' had a history – that is the inescapable inference – which had long since marked him down for punishment when the time was ripe; and the people who enlisted Steinie as their agent knew enough about Leon Beron, his family and his background, to select him as their victim, when a victim was needed, though their own connexion with that background may have been tenuous or non-existent. His death, indeed, was incidental to a larger purpose and part of a more grandiose project: that is the guess I propose to hazard, but exposition of my guess must wait for my next and concluding chapter. In that I shall summon to my help a man more knowledgeable than I, and far more gifted.

Here, at this stage of the narrative – to be precise at this stage of the activities that I believe to have been set in motion by the people who engaged Steinie Morrison as their agent – Steinie became a regular customer at the Warsaw Restaurant. According to the testimony of Joe Mintz, that was on or about 1 December, and from then till the end of the year – if other witnesses can be believed – Steinie and Leon Beron lived in such companionship as the restaurant afforded. On occasion, indeed, their companionship may have found larger, extra-mural dimensions, for Muir, when cross-examining Morrison on Monday, 13 March, had suggested that on 29 or 30 January he had left the Warsaw with Zaltzman, Beron and the old man known as 'the Colonial'; and that Morrison subsequently took Leon Beron to the brothel managed by Hugo Pool. Muir was relying on evidence volunteered by Zaltzman, and as a witness Israel Zaltzman had been proved untrustworthy; but Morrison – who, of course, denied the story – had freely admitted his knowledge of several 'prostitutes' houses', as he called them, and though Snelwar had spoken of Leon Beron's ascetic habit his evidence had been disputed by Leon's brother David.

It is possible, then – one may hazard the guess – that Steinie, having won the confidence of Leon Beron, excited his gratitude by introducing him to pleasures – and footing the bill for them – to which Leon, in his parsimonious way of life, had long been a stranger. Then, to meet a final obligation to his unknown paymasters – whose purpose may have been more deadly than he knew – he introduced Beron, on the last night of the year, to a man of commanding stature and respectable appearance: a man whom he would describe as an old friend in whose tact and *savoir faire* Beron could have perfect confidence. Together they went to one of the brothels with which Steinie was familiar, and there they gave Beron a drink or two, and a couple of ham sandwiches. But his friend, said Steinie – or so one may imagine – knew houses of better entertainment, not too far away, and was, in fact, about to visit one near Clapham Common. Then, perhaps, the friend invited Beron to go with him. They would take a hansom cab, he said, and in the house he knew there were some girls of the most obliging disposition. All doubt dispelled by drink, discretion vanished and Beron was persuaded by intemperate thoughts to drive with an ingratiating stranger to Clapham Common; from where he did not return.

Steinie retired to Newark Street – in his evidence he had again deviated into truth – and, though he arrived somewhat later than the hour named by the Zimmermans, he remained there, peacefully sleeping, till nine or ten in the morning.

At two o'clock, or thereabouts, Hayman the cabman picked up Beron and a tall, well-dressed stranger, and drove them to Lavender Gardens. Near where he set them down, they were joined by a third man, who may or may not have been X, whom at a later date Mrs X attempted to betray. It was he, the third man, who killed Beron.

The stranger, who bore a superficial resemblance to Morrison, hired the cabman Stephens, who drove him to the rank near Kennington Church. There, waiting for him, he found the co-ordinator of the plot – perhaps Peter the Painter himself – and Castlin the taxi-driver took them to Seven Sisters Road and the anarchic security, as Abinger regarded it, of Tottenham. X, if it was he who murdered Beron, had been left on the Common to make a devious way to safety, and did not return home till three days later.

The substance of the last few paragraphs is, of course, guess-work; but it is guess-work that fits the known facts more closely than the case for the prosecution advanced by Mr Muir. I accept Inspector Wensley's assurance that there was no proven association between Leon Beron and the Houndsditch murderers; but I think it probable that there was a connexion, of which Wensley and the police had imperfect knowledge, between the Houndsditch crime, the death on Clapham Common and the affray in Sidney Street. For an explication of that connexion I need another chapter and the assistance of Joseph Conrad, who advanced a very daring theory, not after those events, but some four years before them.

FIFTEEN

IT was in 1907 that Conrad published his novel called *The Secret Agent*, and prefaced it with what must be regarded as an apology for composing a story so startlingly different from its immediate predecessors, which were *Nostromo* and *The Mirror of the Sea*. 'The thought', he wrote, 'of elaborating mere ugliness in order to shock, or even simply to surprise my readers by a change of front, has never entered my head. In making this statement I expect to be believed, not only on the evidence of my general character but also for the reason, which anybody can see, that the whole treatment of the tale, its inspiring indignation and under-lying pity and contempt, prove my detachment from the squalor and sordidness which lie simply in the outward circumstances of the setting.'

The subject, he says – 'I mean the tale' – came to him in the shape of a few words spoken by a friend in the course of casual conversation about anarchists – 'or rather anarchist activities'. Conrad had been saying something about 'the criminal futility of the whole thing', and into his concept of the whole thing he throws, as if it were a waste-paper basket, anarchist doctrine and action, the anarchists' mentality and the brazen, half-crazy dishonesty with which they exploited 'the poignant miseries and passionate credulities of a mankind always so tragically eager for self-destruction'. That was what made, for him, the philosophical pretences of anarchism so unpardonable. Then he or his friend, passing to particular instances, 'recalled the already old story of the attempt to blow up the Greenwich Observatory; a blood-stained inanity of so fatuous a kind that it was impossible to fathom its origin by any reasonable or even unreasonable process of thought'.

From that *impasse* he was rescued by his friend who, after a short silence, 'remarked in his characteristically casual and omniscient manner: "Oh, that fellow was half an idiot. His sister committed suicide afterwards."'

For Conrad those few words had a curiously illuminating quality, so that 'one felt like walking out of a forest on to a plain – there was not much to see but one had plenty of light'. For the ordinary or average person those two short sentences may do very little to dispel the darkness of a forest, but Conrad had more vision than most, and as if in the light of sudden day he saw that a poor human being – half an idiot – could be tempted to blood-stained inanity and self-destruction by processes of thought that defied both reason and unreason. The poor human, moreover, had had a sister who loved him beyond reason; and in the artist's mind pity and indignation began to stir, began to create a cast of pitiable, ungainly characters, and the machinery of a plot that would start some of them on a grotesque road to tragedy.

Conrad was a Pole by birth, an aristocrat or near-aristocrat by breeding. He was magnanimous, but his magnanimity was as severely charted as if he were a sea-captain who knew his way about the world, and knew where he had to go. He had a catholic understanding of men and their world, but his sympathy was selective. He was less tolerant than are the majority of English writers, but perhaps more inclined to give honour to those who had earned it. For those who woke anger or roused his contempt he had little pity, but for the victims of cant and oppression there was pity to spare. Being a Pole, moreover, he had an easier apprehension of the wicked machinations of government – of some governments – than was common to the majority of Englishmen in the reign of Edward VII, and with that knowledge – and a novelist's permitted expansion of it – he built the plot which trapped fat and indolent Mr Verloc in its deadly machinery.

Mr Verloc was his secret agent whose ostensible business was conducted in a small, dingy shop in Soho, the window of which displayed 'photographs of more or less undressed dancing girls; nondescript packages in wrappers like patent medicines' – and 'a few books with titles hinting at impropriety'. A rubber shop that did little trade, for Verloc was a slovenly, idle man who on ordinary occasions 'had an air of having wallowed, fully dressed, all day on an unmade bed'.

He had won, however – and idly enjoyed – the affection, admiration or devotion of Winnie his wife, a young woman with an attractive figure and 'an air of unfathomable indifference'; of Winnie's mother, 'a stout, wheezy woman with a large brown face' who had known better times, considered herself to be of French descent and wore 'a black wig under a white cap'; and of Stevie, Winnie's young brother, who 'was delicate and, in a frail way, good-looking too, except for the vacant droop of his lower lip'. But Stevie was a domestic problem, his intelligence was minimal, and even as an errand-boy he had proved a failure: 'He forgot his messages; he was easily diverted from the straight path of duty by the attractions of stray cats and dogs, which he followed down narrow alleys into unsavoury courts . . . or by the dramas of fallen horses, whose pathos and violence induced him some-times to shriek piercingly in a crowd.'

In the rancid atmosphere of that dingy little house there is a great warmth of love. The two women care for Stevie with a pas-sionate devotion, they are grateful to Verloc for giving them and the boy a good home, and Stevie rewards with his affection all who do not offend him by some display of coldness or cruelty. They are vulnerable to the world's malevolence, and their vul-nerability is exposed and extended by Verloc's slovenly incapa-city, his lazy self-esteem.

He dresses well, however – he shaves cleanly, he smartens himself up – when he goes to meet his foreign employer, and the machinery of the plot begins to purr with a sinister drone when he walks past Hyde Park Corner to the ponderous respectability beyond it. His destination is an Embassy in Chesham Square to which he has been unexpectedly summoned. He is received with the coldness of a flunkey's welcome, and led into the presence of Privy Councillor Wurmt, *Chancellier de l'Ambassade*. He, it is made evident, is Verloc's paymaster, and grimly apparent is the fact that he is ill-pleased with Verloc's work for him. He is, more curiously, dissatisfied with the behaviour of London's policemen.

They are too liberal in their view, too lenient in their dealing with foreign dissidents. 'What is desired', says the Privy Councillor, 'is the occurrence of something definite which should stimulate their vigilance'; and he adds, 'That is within your province – is it not so?'

The Privy Councillor clarifies and expands his statement: 'The vigilance of the police – and the severity of the magistrates. The general leniency of the judicial procedure here, and the utter absence of all repressive measures, are a scandal to Europe. What is wished for just now is the accentuation of the unrest, of the fermentation which undoubtedly exists.'

Verloc attempts to defend himself, and is gently reproved by Wurmt, who says, 'Your reports for the last twelve months have been read by me. I failed to discover why you wrote them at all.'

Verloc is then taken to see Mr Vladimir, First Secretary in the Embassy, a younger man, a favourite in London's diplomatic society, who obviously intends to stand no nonsense from an idle employee; and promptly he berates Verloc, not only for his inefficiency, but for his indecent corpulence. A fat anarchist is both absurd and offensive. Verloc, in his relative youth, was an unsuccessful spy, but for the last eleven years has been drawing pay from the Embassy in Chesham Square. He has a good voice, a famous voice, for open-air meetings and rebellious workmen's assemblies in large halls. But all his rhetorical addresses have achieved nothing. He is an *agent provocateur* who has failed to provoke sufficient anger in his audiences. And now he is faced with the terrifying threat: 'No work, no pay!'

Vladimir reminds him of the International Conference then sitting in Milan, and says, 'What we want is to administer a tonic to the Conference. Its deliberations upon international action for the suppression of political crime don't seem to get anywhere. England lags. This country is absurd with its sentimental regard for individual liberty. . . . The imbecile bourgeoisie of this country make themselves the accomplices of the very people whose aim is to drive them out of their houses to starve in ditches.' The English bourgeoisie must be frightened, says Vladimir; and, to Verloc, 'This is the psychological moment to set your friends to work.'

He explains what is necessary: 'A series of outrages executed here in this country: not only *planned* here – that would not do – they would not mind. Your friends could set half the Continent on fire without influencing the public opinion here in favour of universal repressive legislation.'

That, then, is his aim – universal repressive legislation – and the aim, it must be assumed, of his government or of an influential party within it. The outrages he looks forward to, however, 'need not be especially sanguinary', and, 'as if delivering a scientific lecture', Vladimir goes on to say, 'But they must be sufficiently startling – effective. Let them be directed against buildings, for instance. What is the fetish of the hour that all the bourgeoisie recognise – eh, Mr Verloc?'

In Vladimir's opinion science is that fetish, and a deliberate attack on a building dedicated to science – a temple of science – will be more startling and effective than old-fashioned assassination. Now the whole civilised world has heard of Greenwich, and the target he has in mind – a target for the outrageous violence of dynamite – is the Observatory there.

Verloc is given his ultimatum. He has a month in which to plan and bring about the outrage – or else 'No work, no pay'.

Verloc, in despair, goes off to meet his old anarchist companions, knowing they will not help him. There is Michaelis, a ticket-of-leave man living fatly on the distant memory of a single reckless act he committed in his youth; there is Karl Yundt, an old, bald, toothless 'terrorist' whose terrorism is all his own invention; there is Comrade Ossipon, failed medical student and pamphleteer – none of them is capable of action.

There remains, as a possible ally, an eccentric figure known as 'the Professor'; and Conrad fails entirely to persuade us – in an age that has a more sophisticated knowledge of bombs than the Edwardians enjoyed – that the Professor is a credible figure. He goes about the streets, secure from interference by the police, because he carries in his pockets an explosive mixture, and an improbable detonator activated by the bulb of an old-fashioned motor-horn, that are capable of destroying – if he pressed the bulb – a large room and all the people in it.

Let that pass, however, for every age possesses a scientific or pseudo-scientific knowledge that succeeding ages ridicule and dismiss. It is from the Professor that Verloc procures his dynamite, a bomb that seems to have been as clumsy as a pudding-basin, and as the month that Vladimir allowed him draws to an end he enlists – without intending that he should come to any harm – the delicate, tender-hearted, half-wit boy Stevie, his wife Winnie's beloved brother, and Stevie goes up the hill above Greenwich to the same fearful death that rewarded the insane purpose of Martial Bourdin in February 1894.

The family that had lived so snugly, in the warmth of love, behind the shabby little rubber shop in Soho, is engulfed in total tragedy; but that is not the topic of this chapter. Its topic is the machinery of Conrad's plot, and his apparent belief that a major continental power – which must be identified as Russia – was capable of provoking such an outrage, as Martial Bourdin paid for with his life, not for an anarchic purpose, but to excite 'universal repressive legislation' against anarchism. And naturally one asks, Was such a belief, in the early years of this century, plausible? Was such a policy credible?

We have, in comparatively recent years, agreed to accept a view of history that does less credit to humanity, and those who have governed it, than was common a few generations ago. We have, for example, learnt much about Elizabethan and early Jacobean history that used to lie decently hidden behind official curtains. Few people nowadays refuse to believe that the Babington plot, which finally brought Mary, Queen of Scots, to her death was watched and encouraged, if not originally confected, by Elizabeth's own ministers; and the fame of the Gunpowder Plot has been diminished by strong suspicion that it, too, owed much to the enterprise and sagacity of a government whose purpose was to expose, to their discredit, the dissidence of many English Catholics. In years, moreover, much closer to the present time a multitude of grateful readers have accepted the seeming verisimilitude of stories by such gifted writers as Len Deighton and John le Carré in which double-dealing, and complications of double-dealing, are gradually exposed as the common practice of government agents, no matter what government they represent. It would, of course, be unwise to reward with total credence works designed for popular entertainment, but it would be foolish to deny their influence. It is, in part, due to them that governments and their secret servants are no longer uniformed in official white-wash, but on active service – like other forward troops – wear clothing discreetly dyed to match their background.

I return to the last weeks of 1910 and the first few days of 1911, and look into the records of what happened in Russia, in preced-ing months, to see what there was in its political temper that might have prompted, from Russia itself and from its Embassy in Chesham Square, the bloody violence in Houndsditch and Sidney Street, the mysterious affair on Clapham Common, and linked them – as seems possible – in a common purpose to excite 'universal repressive legislation' against anarchism.

It seems, at first sight, that little or nothing can be found to excuse, explain – still less to justify – a policy so murderous in intention, and in its subterranean execution as elaborately planned as the breaching of a fortress by sap and mine. 1910 was a rela-tively peaceful year in Russia, the principal event being the final formulation of a programme for agrarian reform that had been under discussion for some considerable time. Stolypin was Presi-dent of the Council of Ministers, and with the Octobrists he had created a central party which briefly dominated the political scene, and persuaded or compelled the extreme Right Wing to withdraw from the Duma. But, while the Right Wing opposed reform, the Left accused Stolypin of reaction, and a year later – in September 1911 – he was mortally wounded, at the Opera House in Kiev, by a member of a terrorist organisation, a Jew called Bogrov, who had incautiously been allowed to join the secret police.

Behind a benevolent programme of agrarian reform there were other forces in Russian politics, the strongest of which was a great tide of nationalism. Finland was deprived of its autonomy, and Poland stripped of what small independence it may have enjoyed or pretended to enjoy. 'Russification' had popular support as well as official backing, minorities suffered in consequence and anti-Semitism flourished. Outside the Duma the Right Wing had, perhaps, more influence than within it; and nationalism, un-hampered by constitutional responsibility, may have adopted some unorthodox methods in pursuit of its aim: there have always been those who see, in a promise of safety, prosperity and aggrandisement for their country, an end that justifies any means necessary to attain it.

Were there such nationalists – of so ardent a temper, unrestrained by diplomatic convention – at the Russian Embassy in London? Was there, in Chesham House, a Wurmt or a Vladimir who believed, as did Conrad's characters, that the English bourgeoisie must be given a severe and memorable fright, and anarchism put down by repressive laws? And, if a Wurmt or Vladimir there was, it may seem that his belief and lack of scruple were justified by results. Did the well-armed burglars in Houndsditch deliberately attract defenceless policemen to the house behind a jeweller's shop to shoot them and shock the bourgeoisie? The affray in Sidney Street was apparently the consequence of blunder by imperfectly identified foreign invaders, but their blunder reinforced the fear and horror that had spilled out, like smoke over the besieged house, from a Houndsditch slum. And on Clapham Common there was a murder perfectly designed to leave, as well as a dead body in the darkness, a mystery unresolved by the most urgent enquiry, and a nagging fear of the aliens who had gathered so thickly in London's East End. By three events, each of them outrageous – and their effect multiplied by the rapidity with which they assaulted law and order, peace and decency – the bourgeois blood of England was chilled or curdled. Parliament enacted no repressive legislation, but the Metropolitan Police may have exercised greater vigilance in Whitechapel, Tottenham and other haunts or reputed haunts of continental anarchists; for after the trial of Steinie Morrison violence of foreign origin vanished from the English scene until August 1914, when England and the rest of Britain challenged, a few miles from home, a sort of violence unparalleled in their history.

In 1910 the Russian Ambassador in London was Count Benckendorff, whose Military Attaché was General Yermoloff. Should either of them be blamed, or perhaps congratulated, for the three years of comparative peace that London enjoyed after the flames died down in Sidney Street?

By Eric Linklater

NOVELS
White Maa's Saga
Poet's Pub
Juan in America
The Men of Ness
Magnus Merriman
Ripeness is All
Juan in China
The Sailor's Holiday
The Impregnable Women
Judas
Private Angelo
A Spell for Old Bones
Mr Byculla
Laxdale Hall
The House of Gair
The Faithful Ally
The Dark of Summer
Position at Noon
Roll of Honour
Husband of Delilah
A Man Over Forty
A Terrible Freedom

FOR CHILDREN
The Wind on the Moon
The Pirates in the Deep Green Sea
Karina with Love

SHORT STORIES
God Likes Them Plain
Sealskin Trousers
A Sociable Plover
The Stories of Eric Linklater

AUTOBIOGRAPHY
The Man on My Back
A Year of Space
Fanfare for a Tin Hat

BIOGRAPHY
Ben Jonson and King James
Mary Queen of Scots
Robert the Bruce
The Prince in the Heather

ESSAYS
The Lion and the Unicorn
The Art of Adventure
The Ultimate Viking
Edinburgh
Orkney and Shetland

HISTORY
The Campaign in Italy
The Conquest of England
The Survival of Scotland
The Royal House of Scotland

VERSE
A Dragon Laughed

PLAYS
The Devil's in the News
Crisis in Heaven
To Meet the Macgregors
Love in Albania
The Mortimer Touch
Breakspear in Gascony

CONVERSATIONS
The Cornerstones
The Raft *and* Socrates Asks Why
The Great Ship *and* Rabelais Replies

PAMPHLETS
The Northern Garrisons
The Defence of Calais
The Highland Division
Our Men in Korea
The Secret Larder

207